IN SEARCH
OF PAUL

*Unleashing the Power of
Legendary Mentors in Your Life*

TONY COOKE

"Come near to the holy men and women of the past and you will soon feel the heat of their desire after God. They mourned for Him, they prayed and wrestled and sought for Him day and night, in season and out, and when they found Him, the finding was all the sweeter for the long seeking."

—A. W. Tozer

"Since it is so likely that children will meet cruel enemies, let them at least have heard of brave knights and heroic courage."

—C. S. Lewis

CONTENTS

APPENDIX

INTRODUCTION

I was surprised at the words that came out of my mouth, and even more so at the overwhelming gratitude and joy I felt in my heart. During the writing of this book, my wife, Lisa, asked one day how my morning had gone. I spontaneously responded, "I had the best time with Dietrich Bonhoeffer this morning, and my time with Wesley and Spurgeon yesterday was absolutely amazing." I hope this doesn't sound too weird, because all of those people have long since passed away; they have run their race and gone on to their reward. I am not implying that Spurgeon literally appeared to me or that I had an in-person, face-to-face conversation with Wesley. I have had no Mount of Transfiguration experiences as when Moses and Elijah came and spoke with Jesus.

Here is what I was saying: The *writings* of many great men and women through the centuries are still with us, and we can still benefit immeasurably from the wisdom and spiritual insights they left behind. Some of what these godly ministers said in the last two millennia is presented in an older vernacular, and some of their remarks reflect their unique cultural setting. However, a large percentage of what they say powerfully transcends multiple generations and locales; the eternal principles they share can impart so much wisdom and insight into our lives today.

What if we—as much as a sanctified, spiritual imagination allows—try to step into the shoes (however large they might be)

of the greatest ministers and mentors of all time or, perhaps even more precisely, simply sit *at* their feet? These leaders regularly coached and mentored their students toward godliness, maturity, and effective ministry. Have you ever thought about time travel? How much would you pay if someone invented a machine that allowed us the opportunity to go back in history and ask questions to people like Augustine, Richard Baxter, Jonathan Edwards, D. L. Moody, and Catherine Booth? Imagine the incalculably valuable wisdom they could share with us about spiritual growth and dynamic ministry.

Even more importantly, what if we were to study Paul's letters and other writings from Scripture in such a way that biblical figures also became our spiritual coaches, advisors, and counselors? I am not putting the statements of other individuals from church history on par with the Bible; Scripture is infallible and is our authoritative standard. However, I think we can still acquire tremendous lessons from so many of the seasoned saints who have gone before us.

Speaking of Scripture, Solomon pleaded with his son to hearken unto wisdom and to turn from evil throughout the book of Proverbs. He speaks of how *"wisdom calls out"* and *"cries aloud"* (Proverbs 8:1-3 NLT). Similarly, Martin Luther states, "The Bible is alive, it speaks to me; it has feet, it runs after me; it has hands, it lays hold of me." Pastor Wayne Cordeiro fabulously addresses how lessons imparted from biblical characters can help us on our respective journeys in his great work, *The Divine Mentor*. Cordeiro writes, "All the mentors of the ages await your audience. Don't keep them waiting. Enter the Bible daily, and there will be a dusting of heaven on everything you do."[1]

What Is Ahead?

The first two chapters provide an overview of the dynamic power of *influence* and *example*. It is essential to remember the purpose of this book is not to simply give information, but to facilitate transformation. Not only have we been shaped by the observations we have made over the years, but we also have the ability to become positive influencers through our lifestyle and example. As we develop, we have the privilege and responsibility to help develop others. When we have been positively impacted by those who have preceded us, we have the opportunity to impact others who follow us.

We begin each of the next eight chapters (3–10) by presenting a foundational principle that Paul emphasized in his two epistles to Timothy, his young assistant. After establishing a solid biblical basis for each of these eight principles, I demonstrate how great leaders throughout church history have stressed identical truths to those they were training. Whether you are just beginning to serve God in the ministry of helps, or whether you are a long-tenured preacher, this book is loaded with life-changing and ministry-enhancing truth.

In addition to knowing what this book *is*, it is also good to know what this book is *not*. This is not a verse-by-verse exposition or commentary on 1 and 2 Timothy. Though we refer to many of the things Paul taught Timothy and identify some major themes therein, we are not dealing with these books comprehensively and exhaustively. For example, the qualifications for bishops and deacons (1 Timothy 3:1-13) are of great importance, but I covered that theme in my book *Qualified: Serving God with Integrity and Finishing Your Course with Honor.* Likewise, I have a book entitled *Relationships Matter: Lessons from Paul and the People Who Impacted His Life* in which I go into detail about the varied relationships Paul navigated throughout his ministry. Paul details these in 2 Timothy 4:9-21, so I don't go into those same issues in this book.

Throughout the book, and particularly at the end of chapters, I include Check-Up Questions. This is one of the most important parts of this book. I believe each chapter will challenge you, and you may find some of the standards communicated to be a bit intimidating. If you feel like you don't measure up in some areas, don't get discouraged, quit, or get under condemnation. You don't have the boldness of Luther, have as much discipline as Wesley, preach as well as Spurgeon, evangelize as effectively as Moody, or live as sacrificially as Bonhoeffer? Join the club. We all have room to grow, and that is a major purpose of this book—to spur us to greater development and maturity.

Why *In Search of Paul* as a Title?

So many believers, even preachers, hunger for mentoring and coaching in their own lives. If you have a flesh-and-blood person who provides you such training, you are certainly blessed. That said, please don't compare your pastor or mentor with Paul, Augustine, Edwards, Tozer, and the dozens of other great spiritual leaders we will explore in this book. That sets a most intimidating standard. I don't want to be compared to these leaders, and it is very unfair to ask that level of greatness of others.

If you were a basketball coach, could you imagine if everyone expected you to be the perfect composite of Mike Krzyzewski, Jim Boeheim, Jim Calhoun, Roy Williams, and Bobby Knight?[2] No one coach can embody all of their skill, wisdom, and expertise. With that in mind (for the purpose of this book *title*), the Paul we are searching for is not just the literal, historical apostle of Scripture. Rather, he represents a synthesis of the greatest mentors of all time. I cannot provide you with a time machine to literally travel back and interact with these great people from the Bible or church history, but hopefully this book will offer you profound wisdom from some of the greatest spiritual coaches through history. My prayer is that you develop a profound appreciation for the price these great leaders paid and draw deeply from the well—the amazing treasury—that they left behind for our enrichment and benefit.

Notes

1. Wayne Cordeiro, *The Divine Mentor: Growing Your Faith as You Sit at the Feet of the Savior* (Bloomington, MN: Bethany House Publishers, 2007), 208.

2. At the time of this writing, these are the five winningest coaches in NCAA men's basketball in the United States.

ABOUT THE PREQUEL

W hen *In Search of Timothy: Discovering and Developing Greatness in Church Staff and Volunteers* was released in 2005, I did not appreciate its potential impact. Since that time, it has been translated into several other languages, and a large number of churches stateside and abroad continue using it to train their workers and leaders. Some pastors have told me that it is required reading for anyone who is going to serve in key roles on their team because they appreciate its emphasis on team members having godly attitudes and maintaining a servant's heart.

I have been especially touched by comments from people serving in supportive roles over the years. They have indicated its helpfulness as they have navigated the challenges of working effectively with their pastors and with other members of the team. Several have told me they would have quit had it not been for the instruction and encouragement in that book. In the midst of these interactions, a recurring remark has surfaced: "*In Search of Timothy* was so helpful to me, but have you considered writing a similar book entitled *In Search of Paul*?" The implication has been that Timothy's example and associated principles are helpful in knowing how to serve, but these same individuals also desire to have mentoring from above.

Many leaders and senior pastors have also told me that they sense a great need for guidance and coaching in their own lives. Who wouldn't benefit from wise, sage advice from someone who has been down the road, from someone with far more experience and wisdom? Maybe you have received a lot of great input and counsel during the course of your spiritual journey, and if so, that's great. But maybe you feel a need for more, and that is the purpose of this book. Seeking to become a servant like Timothy and seeking for leadership input like Paul would provide, speaks of our quest for growth. We hunger for constructive input, and we desire growth and development.

You might be inclined to envy the type of relationship Timothy had with Paul. "If only I had a Paul who could sit down with me on a regular basis and just encourage me, coach me, and teach me!" That may sound good, but I wonder how realistic it is. Timothy certainly had some rich times of receiving from Paul, especially as they traveled together. However, it may not have been as idealistic as we think, and Timothy paid a tremendous price for that privilege. One of their early conversations centered around Timothy's need for circumcision (Acts 16:1-3), and this is not something a young man would have relished hearing.

Timothy was also separated from Paul for lengthy periods. Yes, he traveled with Paul at times, but some of Timothy's most important work was done when he was far away from Paul, representing the great apostle in other churches, sometimes on entirely different continents. Paul was not holding Timothy's hand during such seasons, and Paul gave his young protégé some really challenging assignments. Thank God we have the letters that Paul wrote to Timothy; those were desperately needed sources of encouragement to Timothy, and they provide an excellent basis for imagining how Paul might mentor us today.

Chapter One

MOLDED AND SHAPED:

Who Has Influenced You?

"If I have seen further it is by standing on the shoulders of giants."

—*Isaac Newton*

KEY THOUGHT: Much of who we are today is the result of what we have seen, heard, and been exposed to through our lives. Consciously or unconsciously, we filter these experiences, deeming some as admirable and endeavoring to incorporate them into our own lives. Others we reject, resolving not to have such attitudes or actions as a part of who we become.

If you stop and think about it, much of who you are today is an accumulation of countless influences you have been exposed to throughout the course of your life. Of course, you have also been highly impacted by the decisions you made about things you have seen, learned, and experienced. You have likely chosen to embrace and incorporate into your life certain positive influences from your past, and you have also probably rejected other influences and disallowed them a place in your life.

Jonathan Edwards, the famed pastor and theologian during America's Great Awakening, made it a point that if he saw or heard of anything praiseworthy in another person, he would seek to embrace and embody that trait. Likewise, if he was aware of a negative trait in another person, he would determine not to replicate it. Many of us have probably done the exact same thing, perhaps on numerous occasions, although we may not have been as intentional as Edwards was.

When some people think of mentoring, they picture a formal, structured setting. For example, they envision having a weekly meeting with a spiritual leader to study Scripture and discuss life with them. No doubt this type of thing might happen, and it can be a very valid form of promoting spiritual formation in a person's life. However, for every formal situation like this, we probably experience thousands of informal learning opportunities throughout life.

I lived in a very small town (around two thousand people) through my first year of elementary school. One of my vivid memories is being in the front yard with my dad when a car drove by and he waved at the driver.

I remember asking my dad, "Did you know that person?"

He responded, "No, I was just being friendly."

That seems like such a small and insignificant event, but for some reason it made a big impression on me. My dad probably thought absolutely nothing of that moment, but it has stuck with me all these years. Somehow, his small gesture communicated to me that it is a good thing to be friendly and outgoing, and I have endeavored to emulate that throughout my life.

After we moved to a larger city, I was part of a swim team when I was in sixth grade. When my mom picked me up at the YMCA, she noticed a young kid in the lobby who seemed a little lost. She asked

him if he was alright and if he had a way to get home. After consulting with the staff, she offered to give the boy a ride home. He was greatly relieved that someone was willing to help him, and I remember that car ride to this day. Again, it was a life lesson for me—that it is good to be aware of others and to help people in need.

Neither of these situations happened in a classroom setting; they just happened in the course of everyday life. My parents probably were not aware that they were teaching me at those moments, but that's how a large percentage of mentoring takes place—by example. One of my heroes, John Wooden, said, "Mentoring can be any action that inspires another; every time we watch someone and make a mental note about that individual's character or conduct, we're being mentored."[1]

Wooden wrote of different mentors whose examples and influence had dramatically impacted his life. Among those he discussed were his father and his wife, three coaches for whom he had played, and two individuals he had never met: Abraham Lincoln and Mother Teresa. Though Wooden was ninety-eight years old when he wrote that, he spoke of how he was still learning from other people. Having mentored countless individuals throughout his own life, Wooden was passionately committed to both teaching and being taught. He writes:

> The important thing is that you open yourself up to be a willing student. You need to allow yourself the luxury of learning. Sometimes that might even involve swallowing a little pride, but there is nothing more valuable than learning from someone who has been there. Advice, after all, is just experience without the pain of having to learn those lessons yourself.[2]

Howard Hendricks, a professor at Dallas Theological Seminary for sixty years, is another individual who had great insights into the power of mentoring. He writes,

> Mentoring is what happens when one man affects another man deeply enough to where he later declares, "I never would have become who I am were it not for that man's influence."[3]

It is good to sometimes take inventory of who has helped us grow and become better in life. Whether their influence was intentional or incidental, we should always be grateful. Even if the example was a bad one, we can take it as a warning, as a behavior to avoid.

Many years ago, I was speaking at a conference for pastors and church leaders in Brazil. During a question-and-answer session, I was asked about the greatest lesson I had learned from Kenneth E. Hagin, for whom I had worked for more than eighteen years. Brother Hagin was a prolific author and Bible teacher, and at first, I thought I would not be able to provide a concise answer; there were just too many lessons to choose from.

All of a sudden, a key lesson popped into my mind, and I told the audience, "The most important lesson I learned from Brother Hagin is that he always gave his wife the best egg." Perhaps the audience was expecting a profoundly spiritual or theological type of answer, but my response was about an egg. I explained to them that throughout the course of their marriage, Brother Hagin would always go to the kitchen and prepare two eggs while his wife, Oretha, was getting ready in the morning. He would always give her whichever egg looked best, and he ate the other one. This may not sound overly spiritual, but

it made a big impression on me and instilled within me the principle that love prefers the other person.

I also had the privilege of working with Kenneth W. and Lynette Hagin for the same number of years. Serving as an associate pastor, I witnessed their "can do" attitude regularly. Their tenacious approach was based on this premise: We will do whatever it takes to get the job done. They both taught and lived that principle. One day as Pastor Hagin and I were walking into one of the buildings on campus, he saw a small piece of clear cellophane (probably from a candy wrapper) several feet away from where we were walking. Even though it was well out of the way, he walked over, picked it up, and threw it in the trash can once we got into the building.

That may seem insignificant to some, and I'm sure Pastor Hagin did not think one thing about it, but for whatever reason it made a big impression on me. That simple act modeled a servant's heart and expressed the idea: If you see something that needs to be done, do it. It was also an important reminder that you are never too important to do seemingly small things. These types of moments can be mentoring moments, even if they are unintentional. It should remind us that people may be watching more closely than we think, and it also reminds us to have our eyes open to learn at all times.

An Even Bigger Picture

I am guessing that we can all think back through our lives and recall both positive and negative behaviors we saw exhibited by others. Maybe we even had a conscious checklist of positive traits we admired and hoped to emulate or negative attributes we never wanted to incorporate into our own lives. Perhaps we saw these different elements in parents, teachers, coaches, or neighbors, but all of us have been exposed to countless examples throughout life, both positive and negative.

One of the common characteristics of these exposures is that they happened right in front of us. We really didn't have any control over who our parents and other relatives were, where we lived, or where we went to school; all of that was outside of our control. But another type of influence, outside of our native sphere, is found in the exemplary people we seek out and study. Many of these may not even be alive on earth any longer, but their lives and examples are still available to us as powerful tools.

When I was a teenager, I read David Wilkerson's book, *The Cross and the Switchblade*. His courage and commitment to Christ inspired me. Around the same time, I read *Tortured for Christ* by Richard Wurmbrand, a Romanian pastor who spent fourteen years in a communist prison. Again, I was profoundly impacted and was in awe of his perseverance and faith in the midst of severe persecution. Though I was young and inclined to look up to sports heroes, deep inside I saw a virtue in these spiritual leaders that far exceeded athletic or other secular accomplishments. Though it would be a few years after reading these books that I would sense God's call to ministry and consecrate myself accordingly, these accounts were living seeds that were planted in my heart.

And There's Much More

Just as the lives of Wilkerson and Wurmbrand spoke to me, God has many examples and witnesses who can influence and speak powerfully to us. Many of these influencers are embedded within Scripture.

"...Although Abel is long dead, he still speaks to us by his example of faith" (Hebrews 11:4 NLT). No one would take that to mean that Abel is physically and literally speaking to us, but that we can still learn from and be inspired by the example of his faith. We are not alone in our spiritual journeys but, are part of a great and glorious company. Scripture reminds us that *"we are surrounded by such a huge crowd of witnesses to the life of faith"* (Hebrews 12:1 NLT). In this same verse, the Message refers to *"those pioneers who blazed the way"* and refers to *"these veterans cheering us on."*

This same principle is powerfully illustrated in a moving scene from *Remember the Titans.* Coach Herman Boone, played by Denzel Washington, is trying to coach a newly integrated high school football team in the early 1970s, and racial tensions are making his job difficult. In a pre-season training camp, Boone leads his team on a tiring, late-night run, and without the team knowing, they end up right next to Gettysburg. As the players try to catch their breath from the exhausting run, Coach Boone dramatically states:

> This is where they fought the battle of Gettysburg. Fifty thousand men died right here on this field, fighting the same fight that we are still fighting among ourselves today. This green field right here, painted red, bubblin' with the blood of young boys. Smoke and hot lead pouring right through their bodies. Listen to their souls, men. "I killed my brother with malice in my heart. Hatred destroyed my family." You listen, and you take a lesson from the dead. If we don't come together right now on this hallowed ground, we too will be destroyed, just like they were. I don't care if you like each other or not, but you will respect each

> other. And maybe... I don't know, just maybe we'll
> learn to play this game like men.[4]

So, the idea of drawing inspiration, lessons, and insight from the writings and lives of those who have gone before us is commonly understood and expressed, both biblically and secularly.

When it comes to our lives, relative to the grand scheme of God's plan, this concept becomes especially powerful when we begin to see ourselves as actual participants in the overall process and not mere spectators. In other words, we no longer simply admire these heroes from a distance, but realize that we are called to be a part of the same journey and to carry the same torch. Billy Graham acknowledged his place in God's overall plan relative to those who preceded him:

> I realize that my ministry would someday come to
> an end. I am only one in a glorious chain of men and
> women God has raised up through the centuries to
> build Christ's church and take the Gospel everywhere.[5]

You and I are links in the same chain, and we should never lose sight of the privilege of being vitally connected to those who came before us, knowing that *"Jesus is not ashamed to call them his brothers and sisters"* (Hebrews 2:11 NLT). We carry a torch that many before us have carried, and we should carry it respectfully and honorably.

When the author of Hebrews mentions the great crowd of witnesses, it is a reference to the legendary Old Testament figures listed in the previous chapter (Noah, Abraham, Sarah, Moses, David, etc.). While we should never diminish the value and significance of those biblical heroes, more than two thousand years have come and gone, and many other heroes of faith have finished their races and taken their place in the grandstands as well. Fortunately for us, many of these not only left remarkable examples, but also powerful, compelling, and inspirational words.

As I mentioned in the Introduction, I am inviting you (figuratively) to be a time traveler with me as you peruse these pages. What would Luther, Wesley, Moody, and Spurgeon say to us if we could sit down and talk with them? What lessons could we glean if we had the privilege of being mentored by them? What if they—from their tremendous journeys of faith—could share their wisdom, experiences, and insights? No, we won't literally travel back in time to visit with them, but their words have traveled into our day and age to encourage, enlighten, and empower us.

When well-known people pass from the scene, we have a tendency to place them on lofty pedestals and to focus only on the bright spots of their lives. It is fitting that we remember their accomplishments, but if we fail to recognize the intense struggles and disappointments such individuals encountered, they will seem distant and unrelatable to us; they remain somehow out of reach. Perhaps this is why James—in mentioning some of Elijah's miracles—states, *"Elijah was as human as we are"* (James 5:17 NLT). The Passion Translation renders it, *"Elijah was a man with human frailties, just like all of us."*

The leaders referred to in this book drew from the same redeeming and empowering grace from which we are privileged to partake. Their Fountain is our Fountain. They had no free passes or easy roads any more than we do. They were not infallible human beings any more than we are. Our allegiance, of course, is to the One perfect person, the Lord Jesus Christ, but we also owe a great debt to those less-than-perfect individuals who blazed the trail before us. Paul preached that David *"served God's purpose in his own generation"* (Acts 13:36 NASB). Should we do any less? Arthur Wallis admonished, "If you would do the best with your life, find out what God is doing in your generation and throw yourself wholly into it."

If you want to run like a champion, train with other champions. Study them. Learn their values. Find out what motivated them. Discover how they overcame their frailties and disadvantages and learned how to trust and obey God in the face of insurmountable odds. As Solomon admonished, *"Walk with the wise and become wise..."* (Proverbs 13:20 NLT). It would seem such a terrible waste to not access the vast riches of wisdom from those who have gone before us, and to that end, I have compiled the chapters that follow.

The Greats Speak on Influence

Oswald Sanders

> "The leader should read to have fellowship with great minds. Through books we hold communion with the greatest spiritual leaders of the ages."[6]

Oswald Chambers

> "If you are going to be a worker for the cure of souls, God will bring you under masters and teachers."

A. W. Tozer

> "Come near to the holy men and women of the past and you will soon feel the heat of their desire after God. They mourned for Him, they prayed and wrestled and sought for Him day and night, in season and out, and when they found Him, the finding was all the sweeter for the long seeking."

Check-Up Questions

Which people have had the most influence on your development over the years? Who set examples and patterns of behavior before you that you have imitated or rejected? Are there specific examples now of character and actions that you have seen that you endeavor to emulate even more?

Notes

1. John Wooden and Don Yaeger, *A Game Plan for Life: The Power of Mentoring* (New York: Bloomsbury USA, 2009), 3.

2. Ibid., 6.

3. Bill Hendricks and Howard Hendricks, *Men of Influence: The Transformational Impact of Godly Mentors* (Chicago: Moody Publishers, 2019), 61.

4. Bruckheimer, J. (Producer), Yakin, B. (Director). (2000). *Remember the Titans* [Motion Picture]. United States: Buena Vista Pictures.

5. Russ Busby, *Billy Graham, God's Ambassador: A Celebration of His Life and Ministry* (San Diego: Tehabi Books, 1999), 18.

6. Oswald Sanders, *Spiritual Leadership: A Commitment to Excellence for Every Believer* (Chicago: Moody Publishers, 2007), Kindle edition, 1960.

Chapter Two

PAUL'S METHOD:

Leading by Example

"You teach a little by what you say. You teach most by what you are."

—*Henrietta Mears*

KEY THOUGHT: The apostle Paul was proactive, intentional, and deliberate in leading by example. Paul did not take the easy route by communicating, "Do as I say, not as I do." With reliance upon the Holy Spirit, Paul modeled godliness and spirituality as an essential part of his life and ministry.

Have you ever stopped to think about the dynamics of why people follow certain leaders? What is it that attracts people to different ones? This may be fairly simplistic, but here are three factors that go into the equation of why a person might be drawn to place himself under another's leadership. They are:

- He believes in that leader's character (He admires who the leader *is*).

- He believes in that leader's communication (He appreciates what the leader *says*).
- He believes in that leader's conquests (He respects what the leader *accomplishes*).

We have all probably heard stories about individuals who were eloquent speakers or accomplished great things, but their character—their personal life—was tragically out of order. In such cases, we can appreciate what a particular leader says and respect what they accomplish, but we probably don't want to be *like* them.

If God has graced you to be an eloquent or powerful speaker, that is great. If you have had great achievements and accomplishments in your life, I am happy for you. Those elements can cause people to notice you, but those elements by themselves don't guarantee that you will have the kind of lasting impact in the lives of others that you might desire; much of that comes from your character—from the quality of person that you are. The epitome of godly character is reflected in what has been referred to as Paul's Love Chapter.

If I could speak all the languages of earth and of angels, but didn't love others, I would only be a noisy gong or a clanging cymbal. If I had the gift of prophecy, and if I understood all of God's secret plans and possessed all knowledge, and if I had such faith that I could move mountains, but didn't love others, I would be nothing. If I gave everything I have to the poor and even sacrificed my body, I could boast about it; but if I didn't love others, I would have gained nothing (1 Corinthians 13:1-3 NLT).

That sets a towering standard. It seems like it is pretty easy to *"be nothing"* and *"gain nothing"* if we do not have the right character—if we do not walk in the love of God.

We should never think that we are the ultimate Christian or the perfect exemplary minister; we always have room for improvement (and so does everyone we admire). However, it is absolutely vital that we understand the importance of our example and how often it carries more influence than our words. In all likelihood, Paul had been deeply impressed by his mentor, Gamaliel, who was *"respected by all the people"* (Acts 5:34 NLT). When the apostle was giving his personal testimony in Jerusalem, he made it a point to stress that he had been brought up *"at the feet of Gamaliel"* (Acts 22:3 NKJV). Paul knew how highly respected his mentor was.

Just as the revered rabbi had modeled the principles of Judaism to his students, Paul sought to demonstrate the substance and reality of Christ's life to Timothy and the churches he established; he was fully intentional in his quest to live an exemplary life. After referring to his sinful past, Paul told Timothy that *"God had mercy on me so that Christ Jesus could use me as **a prime example** of his great patience with even the worst sinners"* (1 Timothy 1:16 NLT). That phraseology is significant. What had happened in Paul's life was not meant to impress people with himself or with how wonderful he was, but rather, to dynamically impact them with how merciful and compassionate God had been.

If we take some creative liberty and consolidate various statements Paul made into a topical paragraph, it becomes clear how important exemplary living was to the great apostle:

> *Timothy, imitate me, just as I also imitate Christ* (1 Corinthians 11:1 NKJV).

Don't let anyone think less of you because you are young. Be an example to all believers in what you say, in the way you live, in your love, your faith, and your purity (1 Timothy 4:12 NLT).

You must remain faithful to the things you have been taught. You know they are true, for you know you can trust those who taught you, and that from childhood you have known the Holy Scriptures (2 Timothy 3:14-15 NLT).

You have closely followed my example and the truth that I've imparted to you. You have modeled your life after the love and endurance I've demonstrated in my ministry by not giving up. The faith I have, you now have. What I have hungered for in life has now become your longing as well. The patience I have with others, you now demonstrate. And the same persecutions and difficulties I have endured, you have also endured (2 Timothy 3:10-11 TPT).

Keep putting into practice all you learned and received from me—everything you heard from me and saw me doing. Then the God of peace will be with you (Philippians 4:9 NLT).

These verses not only demonstrate the transformational power of Paul's godly example, but also of those who had taught Timothy from childhood—this would have included his grandmother Lois and his mother Eunice (2 Timothy 1:5).

One of Paul's statements—*you know you can trust those who taught you*—reminds me of something I experienced very early in my ministry. Our church was having our regular dinner before the Wednesday evening service, and I was mingling with and greeting the people. At one of the tables was a group of senior citizens, and a very dear lady asked me a question. She told me that she had heard two preachers contradict each other earlier in the day on the radio, and it troubled her. She told me their two positions on that particular topic and asked me what I believed to be true.

The teacher in me wanted to take her through various Scripture to show her *how* to think through the matter biblically, but she kindly shut me down. She said something like, "Brother Cooke, I know how you live, and I know that you love Jesus and are close to God. I don't really want to know all the technical information. I just want you to tell me what you believe about that, and whatever you believe will be good for me, too." I appreciated her kind remarks, and I shared my perspective with her, but I would have preferred her to be like the Bereans who *"searched the Scriptures daily"* (Acts 17:11 NKJV).

That experience made me realize the importance of my example, that my lifestyle can either lend credibility toward or detract from what I teach. I understand that the Bible is true whether I embody or express its principles through my own life or not, but people tend to judge spiritual matters based on how proponents of a belief conduct themselves. This is why D. L. Moody said, "Out of 100 men, one will read the Bible, the other 99 will read the Christian." Objective truth is vital, but truth often impacts people most effectively when it is embodied and expressed through believers.

There is danger of course, if we look to someone to always interpret and personify God's truth perfectly; humans will (predictably) fail. No one has ever manifested God's nature and character perfectly except the Lord Jesus Christ. This is why Howard Hendricks wisely said, "When you see me stop following Christ, stop following me." This doesn't mean you need to disassociate from every imperfect person, but it does mean that you shouldn't emulate people's flaws. Rather, make Jesus your ultimate example. This is also why Paul never gave an unqualified and absolute directive for people to follow him. Rather, he instructed, *"Be ye followers of me, even as I also am of Christ"* (1 Corinthians 11:1 KJV). Though Paul realized he was less than perfect and was still growing, he did strive to follow Christ consistently, which is why he also never said, "Do as I say, not as I do."

Paul was also mindful of his responsibility as a role model when he admonished the Philippian church to *"pattern your lives after mine, and learn from those who follow our example"* (Philippians 3:17 NLT). Clearly, Paul believed in teaching the word, but he also put significant emphasis on modeling the word and the power of that influence.

Paul's mindset regarding being an example did not just apply to ethereal, abstract concepts, but also to the very practical elements of life, such as our work ethic. To one church, Paul writes:

> *For you know that you ought to imitate us. We were not idle when we were with you. We never accepted food from anyone without paying for it. We worked hard day and night so we would not be a burden to any of you. We certainly had the right to ask you to feed us, but we wanted to give you an example to follow. Even while we were with you, we gave you this command: "Those unwilling to work will not get to eat"* (2 Thessalonians 3:7-10 NLT).

It seems from the preponderance of biblical principles that the best way to teach something is to do it. Our words should simply illuminate and reinforce what we are living.

The Greats Speak on the Power of Example

Gregory of Nazianzus

Speaking of Basil of Caesarea, Gregory said, "His words were like thunder because his life was like lightning."

Augustine of Hippo

"What I live by, I impart."

Gregory the Great

"The spiritual leader should always be the first to act, that by his lifestyle he may demonstrate the way of life to those who are under his care, and that the flock, which follows the voice and conduct of their shepherd, may learn how to walk better through his example even more than by his words. The leader's position requires him to speak the highest things and he is compelled accordingly to demonstrate the highest things through his life. The shepherd's voice more readily penetrates the hearer's heart when the words spoken are backed up by the life he lives."

"No one should enter into spiritual leadership who does not practice in life what he has learned by study."

"It is certain that no one does more harm in the church than one who has a title and position relating to godliness, and yet lives perversely."

Martin Luther

> "The defects in a preacher are soon spied; let a preacher be endued with ten virtues, and but one fault, yet this one will eclipse and darken all of his virtues and gifts, so evil is the world in these times."

Henry M. Stanley (on observing David Livingstone)

> "When I saw the unwearied patience, that unflagging zeal, those enlightened sons of Africa, I became a Christian at his side, though he never spoke to me about it."

Albert Schweitzer

> "Example is not the main thing in influencing others. It is the only thing."

Matthew Henry

> "Those who teach by their doctrine must teach by their life, or else they pull down with one hand what they build up with the other."

Thomas Brooks

> "A preacher's life should be a commentary of his doctrine; his practice should be a counterpart of his sermons. Heavenly doctrines should always be adorned with a heavenly life."
>
> "The lives of ministers oftentimes convince more strongly than their words; their tongues may persuade, but their lives command."

Jonathan Edwards

> "The same things that ministers recommend to their hearers in their doctrine, they should also show them an example of in their practice."[1]

Richard Baxter

> "Take heed to yourselves, lest your example contradict your doctrine, and lest you lay such stumbling-blocks before the blind, as may be the occasion of their ruin; lest you unsay with your lives, what you say with your tongues; and be the greatest hindrances of the success of your own labors."

Charles Spurgeon

"Our whole life must be such as to add weight to our words..."

D. L. Moody

"A man may preach with the eloquence of an angel, but if he doesn't live what he preaches, and act out in his home and his business what he professes, his testimony goes for naught, and the people say it is all hypocrisy after all; it is all a sham. Words are very empty, if there is nothing back of them."[2]

"The eyes of the world are upon us. They don't read the Bible, but they read you and me, and we talk more by our walk than in any other way. We are 'living epistles, known and read of all men.'"[3]

"Where one man reads the Bible, a hundred read you and me. That is what Paul meant when he said we were to be living epistles, known and read of all men... If we do not commend the Gospel to people by our holy walk and conversation, we shall not win them to Christ. Some little act of kindness will perhaps do more to influence them than any number of long sermons."[4]

A. B. Simpson

> "The best edition of the Holy Scriptures is a holy life. God wants to translate His supernatural book into the living experience of all His children. When someone said to Sir Walter Scott that he was going to write a book, he answered, 'Be a book.'"[5]
>
> "A consistent life and a holy example are the most potent factors in every ministry... The true minister will always live first what he preaches. The most spiritual messages will be neutralized without a holy life."[6]
>
> "We sometimes meet men who impress us not so much with their own personality as with the presence of God which they carry with them."[7]

Dietrich Bonhoeffer

> "One act of obedience is worth a hundred sermons."
>
> "Your life as a Christian should make non-believers question their disbelief in God."

A. W. Tozer

> "It is one thing for a minister to choose a powerful text, expound it and preach from it—it is quite something else for the minister to honestly and genuinely live forth the meaning of the Word from day to day."

Warren Wiersbe

> "The work that the pastor does cannot be separated from the life that he lives. A man may be a successful surgeon and, at the same time, a compulsive gambler; or he may teach algebra with great success and get drunk every weekend. But the man in the ministry reproduces after his kind. This is why Paul warned Timothy, 'Take heed unto thyself, and unto the doctrine...' (1 Timothy 4:16). Bad character can never live with good doctrine. Unless the truth is written on the pastor's heart and revealed in his life, he can never write it on the heart of others."[8]

Bruce Wilkinson

> "Teachers impact more by their character and commitment than by their communication."[9]

Check-Up Questions

Assuming that example comprises a large percentage of what we actually convey to others, how are you doing in that regard? Can you cite any examples by which you are intentionally modeling certain principles or lessons to others? Are you, in any area of your life, contradicting what you say verbally through your example?

Notes

1. Jonathan Edwards, "The True Excellency of a Gospel Minister," *The Works of Jonathan Edwards*, Volume 2 (Edinburgh, UK: The Banner of Truth Trust, 1974), 958.

2. D. L. Moody, *Moody's Stories: Incidents and Illustrations* (Chicago: Moody Publishers, 1899), 77.

3. *Northfield Echoes: A Report of the Northfield Conferences for 1897*, vol 4, ed. Delavan L. Pierson (East Northfield, MA: Northfield Echoes, 1897), 320.

4. D. L. Moody, *The Overcoming Life and Other Sermons* (New York: Fleming H. Revell Company, 1896), Kindle edition, 7077.

5. A. B. Simpson, *Present Truths or the Supernatural*, Kindle edition, 15.

6. A. B. Simpson, "1 and 2 Peter: Ministers of Christ," *The Articles and Sermons of A. B. Simpson*, Kindle edition, 28603.

7. A. B. Simpson, *Present Truths or the Supernatural*, Kindle edition, 28.

8. Warren Wiersbe, *Listening to the Giants* (Grand Rapids: Baker, 1980), 345.

9. Bruce Wilkinson, *The Seven Laws of the Learner: Textbook Edition* (Sisters, OR: Multnomah Press, 1992), 38.

Chapter Three

STAY PUT:

Even When You Feel Like Running

"Stay there in Ephesus."

—1 Timothy 1:3 NLT

> K EY THOUGHT: Can you stay long enough in the right place, even when it is hard? Are you impatient and likely to leave prematurely, before God's purpose for that season of your life has been fulfilled?

"The grass is always greener on the other side." At least that's the message of the old adage. Timothy probably noticed many lush fields (elsewhere) while he was serving Paul. We can experience a strong pull to think that someone else has it better, has a more exciting life, has better circumstances, etc. The constant appeal of a better "somewhere else" means that believers and ministers must sometimes exercise diligence and maturity to stay where they are. Focus and patience are required to cultivate the good where one, is instead of daydreaming about where one is not.

The ability to stay put in the midst of trying circumstances—to not turn tail and run—is one of the traits that will serve believers and ministers well. Adversity and fear are two factors that can cause an individual to want to relocate, but not the only ones. Disappointment from unrealistic expectations or simple impatience can also create an urge to leave and go elsewhere. We don't want to be impulsive and erratic—constantly leaving places before we should.

There are right times and right reasons to make transitions, but too often, people leave prematurely and for wrong reasons. We can adapt Solomon's line of thought from Ecclesiastes chapter three and say, "There is a time to stay put, and a time to leave." I have had a few transitions throughout four decades of ministry, but I have always endeavored to give 100 percent effort while I have been in a particular position. No one should ever feel condemned for making a transition, but when we do make a change, we want to do so gracefully, constructively, and for good reasons.

This brings us to Paul's admonition for Timothy to stay at his post in Ephesus. Paul's own departure from that city is not one of the warmer, more tender scenes in Scripture. When the apostle left the leading city of Asia Minor after the massive riot described in Acts 19, he was very fortunate to be getting out alive. The atmosphere of Ephesus was like an angry hornet's nest, and yet years later, Timothy was assigned to be Paul's representative there. His full statement to Timothy was, *"When I left for Macedonia, I urged you to **stay there in Ephesus** and stop those whose teaching is contrary to the truth"* (1 Timothy 1:3 NLT).

Earlier, it had looked like Timothy was going to have an easier route. When pressure started to intensify in Ephesus (and before the huge riot even took place), Paul had *"sent his two assistants, Timothy and Erastus, ahead to Macedonia while he stayed awhile longer in the province of Asia"* (Acts 19:22 NLT). Little did Timothy realize that years later he would be recommissioned to this strategic city with an assignment to pick up many broken pieces and establish an orderly ministry in a very turbulent environment.

Understandably, many want an easy job in a comfortable environment, but God will sometimes put us in tough positions because we are needed to help turn around problem situations. I can only imagine what Timothy might have thought. "That's great, Paul. You get to go see Lydia and all the believers who love you in Philippi—the ones who support you financially and will show you kindness and hospitality. Meanwhile, you are asking me to stay and deal with all of the problems here." And really, that's exactly what Paul was asking of Timothy.

The pressure cooker in which Paul was asking Timothy to stay is revealed in Paul's reflection on his own experience in Ephesus. He referred to having fought *"wild beasts"* there (1 Corinthians 15:32), and also states:

> *We think you ought to know, dear brothers and sisters, about the trouble we went through in the province of Asia. We were crushed and overwhelmed beyond our ability to endure, and we thought we would never live through it. In fact, we expected to die...* (2 Corinthians 1:8-9 NLT).

Regardless of the turbulence and pressure that existed in Ephesus, Paul asked Timothy to stay there and be part of the solution.

Some might think, "If I could just have a Paul in my life, that would be great." That might be true, but what happens when that "Paul" asks you to do something that totally stretches you—that takes you completely out of your comfort zone. Long before the difficult assignment in Ephesus, Paul had asked his assistant to undergo circumcision—not because Timothy needed it for his salvation or personal benefit—but so that Timothy's ministry to the Jews would be unhindered (Acts 16:3). Paul also left his other spiritual son, Titus, in Crete to minister among *"liars, cruel animals, and lazy gluttons"* (Titus 1:12) and asked him to complete the work that had begun there.

Paul knew that getting the job done meant that the right people not only had to *be* in the right place, but also had to *stay* in the right place. Paul had a painful experience along these lines early in his ministry when Mark abandoned his post, refusing to assist him and Barnabas. In the midst of their first missionary journey, Mark quit and went back to his home in Jerusalem. Later, when Barnabas wanted to give Mark another chance, Paul opposed the idea.

> *But Paul disagreed strongly, since John Mark had deserted them in Pamphylia and had not continued with them in their work* (Acts 15:38 NLT).

Though Mark eventually redeemed himself and came back into Paul's good graces, there was a time when Paul did not consider Mark to be reliable because he had not stayed steady in his position on the apostolic team.

Winston Churchill understood that in order for Great Britain to prevail in the great struggle of WWII, they needed a concerted effort, and many people would have to be in the right place, stay put, and continue doing their jobs! Energy, of course, was indispensable to the war effort, and one time when the coal miners needed inspiration, Churchill spoke to them of the nation's future victory. He said that future generations would inquire as to what roles different ones had played. He then cited how some would speak of their efforts as fighter pilots, in the submarines, as soldiers, and as merchant seamen. The prime minister then spoke directly to the miners: "And you, in your turn, will say, with equal pride and with equal right: "WE CUT THE COAL."

Just like Paul had told Timothy that he needed to stay in Ephesus, Churchill was telling the colliers that they need to stay in the mines. Others may have had more glamorous positions or desirable jobs, but their ability to stay put was essential to the survival and success of the nation. Likewise, in so many spheres of life, people need to learn to stay put and bloom where they are planted. We understand the word *stick-to-itiveness* to mean "intense perseverance" and "tenacity."

Paul's Prescription for Timothy

Not only did Paul tell Timothy that he was to stay put in Ephesus, but he also provided him with some amazing insight on how to do that.

> *...With the strength God gives you, be ready to suffer with me for the sake of the Good News* (2 Timothy 1:8 NLT).

> *Timothy, my dear son, be strong through the grace that God gives you in Christ Jesus...Endure suffering along with me, as a good soldier of Christ Jesus. Soldiers don't get tied up in the affairs of civilian life, for then they cannot please the officer who enlisted them. And athletes cannot win the prize unless they follow the rules. And hardworking farmers should be the first to enjoy the fruit of their labor. Think about what I am saying. The Lord will help you understand all these things* (2 Timothy 2:1, 3-7 NLT).

First, Paul tells Timothy to be strong through God's grace and to endure suffering. Then he uses three metaphors to illustrate necessary traits in serving God: soldiers, athletes, and farmers. While Paul highlights different lessons from each of these roles, they all require toughness and tenacity.

Staying put involves more than just being in a place physically. Some people are physically present, but their hearts are elsewhere. Some have checked out mentally, and they are just going through the motions where they are. Wherever we are, we should be mentally, emotionally, and spiritually engaged. We should give our best where we are, not just daydream about some other place we would rather be.

In addition, staying put implies being vigilant toward and placing high value upon one's specific assignment.

> *Timothy, guard what God has entrusted to you...* (1 Timothy 6:20 NLT).

> *Through the power of the Holy Spirit who lives within us, carefully guard the precious truth that has been entrusted to you* (2 Timothy 1:14 NLT).

One commentator says this word *entrust* "was used in the ancient world of the high obligation of having in trust another person's treasured possession, of keeping it safe, and of returning it as it was."[1] Staying put means that we regard as a sacred trust whatever it is that God has entrusted to us, and this includes the ministry he has given to us and the truth he has placed in our hearts.

"Staying Put" Elsewhere in Scripture

Perhaps one of the highest commendations of staying put is found in Jesus' contrast of the shepherd and the hireling. After identifying himself as the good shepherd who sacrifices his life for the sheep, Jesus states:

> *A hired hand will run when he sees a wolf coming. He will abandon the sheep because they don't belong to him and he isn't their shepherd. And so the wolf attacks them and scatters the flock. The hired hand runs away because he's working only for the money and doesn't really care about the sheep* (John 10:12-13 NLT).

The person that Jesus describes as a shepherd is committed to the welfare of the flock no matter what comes; he or she is not just involved when it is comfortable and convenient. Part of staying put is based on your genuine and deep care for people—that you are committed to being with them even through difficult times.

Two Old Testament stories speak powerfully to the idea of staying put—of not running away from one's assigned place. The first one involves a courageous individual by the name of Shammah:

> *Next in rank was Shammah son of Agee from Harar. One time the Philistines gathered at Lehi and attacked the Israelites in a field full of lentils. The Israelite army fled, but Shammah held his ground in the middle of the field and beat back the Philistines. So the LORD brought about a great victory* (2 Samuel 23:11-12 NLT).

I believe that two things make this story so commendable. First, Shammah stood his ground when everyone else left. You need to make the determination that you will be faithful whether anyone else is or not. The fact that many may be less than faithful is not an excuse for you to not give your best.

Second, Shammah was not faithful in guarding a field full of diamonds or gold; he was faithful defending lentils (similar to beans). Perhaps the ones who fled thought lentils were not worth defending, but Shammah was faithful to the Lord. Some people theorize that they will be faithful when God gives them a really important assignment, but God values it when we are faithful in seemingly small things.

In another Old Testament story, David and his men were pursuing of a band of raiders who had not only stolen their possessions but had also kidnapped their wives and children. Some of David's men became exhausted, so they stayed put and guarded the equipment. When David and his men overtook the raiders and reclaimed their families and their possessions, David insisted that those who stayed behind, guarding the equipment, receive the same reward as those who had gone on the expedition.

> ..."We share and share alike—those who go to battle and those who guard the equipment." From then on David made this a decree and regulation for Israel, and it is still followed today (1 Samuel 30:24-25 NLT).

Sometimes it seems like those who are sent out have a more glamorous assignment than those who stay put, but both roles are vital.

The Greats Speak on Staying Put

D. L. Moody

"The fiercest attacks are made on the strongest forts, and the fiercer the battle the young believer is called on to wage, the surer evidence it is of the work of the Holy Spirit in his heart. God will not desert him in his time of need, any more than He deserted His people of old when they were hard pressed by their foes."[2]

Charles Spurgeon

"Between this and heaven there may be rougher weather yet, but it is all provided for by our covenant Head. In nothing let us be turned aside from the path which the divine call has urged us to pursue. Come fair or come foul, the pulpit is our watch-tower, and the ministry our warfare; be it ours, when we cannot see the face of our God, to trust under THE SHADOW OF HIS WINGS."[3]

"A gentleman who wants an easy life should never think of occupying the Christian pulpit, he is out of place there, and when he gets there the only advice I can give him is to get out of it as soon as possible."[4]

Dietrich Bonhoeffer

> "The messengers of Jesus will be hated to the end of time. They will be blamed for all the division which rend cities and homes. Jesus and his disciples will be condemned on all sides for undermining family life, and for leading the nation astray; they will be called crazy fanatics and disturbers of the peace. The disciples will be sorely tempted to desert their Lord. But the end is also near, and they must hold on and persevere until it comes. Only he will be blessed who remains loyal to Jesus and his word until the end."[5]

William Barclay

> "Endurance is not just the ability to bear a hard thing, but to turn it into glory."

Donald Gee

> "The hireling flees, looks after his own skin, secures his own comfort, and cares not that the sheep may be 'scattered,' and perhaps worse."[6]

Oswald Sanders

> "Most Bible characters met with failure, and survived. Even when the failure was immense, those that found leadership again refused to lie in the dust and bemoan their tragedy.[7]

John Wesley

John Wesley wrote guidelines for those that worked with him in his extensive ministry. It is clear that he expected those laboring under his supervision do as they were directed to do.

> Act in all things, not according to your own will, but as a son in the Gospel. As such, it is your part to employ your time in the manner which we direct; partly, in preaching and visiting from house to house; partly, in reading, meditation, and prayer. Above all, if you labor with us in our Lord's vineyard, it is needful that you should do that part of the work which we advise, at those times and places which we judge most for his glory.[8]

Just like Paul expected Timothy and Titus to do as he directed, Wesley believed the workers under his supervision were to be and stay in their assigned places, faithfully fulfilling their responsibilities.

John Stott

> "You will notice Paul begins, 'But as for you.' This expression is found several times in both 1 and 2 Timothy. It indicates that Timothy was called to be different, as we are called to be different from the world around us: different from the prevailing culture. Timothy was not to drift with the stream... He was not to bend before the pressure of public opinion. He was not to be like a reed shaken with the wind. No, he must take his stand firmly for Jesus Christ, not like a reed, but like a rock in a mountain stream. For he was a *man of God*... False teachers were men and women of the world. They derived their standards from the world around them. But men and women of God derived their values and standards from God Himself. And that's why Timothy was called to be—a man of God."[9]

Check-Up Questions

How are you at staying put? Have you ever left a place or situation too early and regretted it? What did you learn? How are you doing in terms of staying focused on your current assignment and guarding what has been entrusted to you?

Notes

1. George W. Knight Knight III, *The Pastoral Epistles: A Commentary on the Greek Text, New International Greek Testament Commentary* (Grand Rapids, MI; Carlisle, England: W.B. Eerdmans; Paternoster Press, 1992), 276.

2. D. L. Moody, *The Overcoming Life* (Chicago: Moody Publishers, 1994), 10.

3. Charles Spurgeon, *Lectures to My Students* (Louisville: GLH Publishing, 1875), Kindle edition, 218.

4. Charles Spurgeon, *Counsel for Christian Workers*, Kindle edition, 495.

5. Dietrich Bonhoeffer, *The Cost of Discipleship* (New York: Touchstone 2012), Kindle edition, 215.

6. Donald Gee, *Concerning Shepherds and Sheepfolds: A Series of Studies Dealing with Shepherds and Sheepfolds* (London: Elim Publishing Company, 1952), 3.

7. Oswald Sanders, *Spiritual Leadership: A Commitment to Excellence for Every Believer* (Chicago: Moody Publishers, 2007), Kindle edition, 2564.

8. John Wesley, "Minutes of Several Conversations Between the Rev. Mr. Wesley and Others, from the Year 1744, to the year 1799" in *Wesley's Works,* Vol. VIII (Grand Rapids: Baker, 1979), 309-10.

9. John Stott, "A Charge to a Man of God," *The Greatest Sermons Ever Preached*, compiled by Tracey D. Lawrence (Nashville: W Publishing Group, 2005), 131-32.

Chapter Four

THE MAN IN THE MIRROR:
Taking Heed to Yourself

"Take heed to yourselves, lest you perish while you call upon others
to take heed of perishing, and lest you famish yourselves
while you prepare their food."

—Richard Baxter

KEY THOUGHT: Spiritual leaders and Christian workers must be diligent concerning their own spiritual health and vitality. Ministry is not merely outward performance, but is comprised of life flowing from within the vessel.

The simple act of looking in the mirror can present some interesting thoughts. A person doesn't want to do it too much or too little. We would be concerned if someone was constantly looking at himself or herself. Are they vain and self-absorbed? A narcissist? Are they insecure? Similarly, it is not considered a good thing for individuals to never look in a mirror. Are they neglecting proper grooming or indifferent about their appearance? James illustrates truth about hearing and obeying God's word by saying, *"For if you listen to the word and*

*don't obey, it is like **glancing at your face in a mirror**. You see yourself, walk away, and forget what you look like"* (James 1:23-24 NLT).

Likewise, Paul speaks about the importance of believers examining themselves in both Corinthian letters (1 Corinthians 11:28, 31; 2 Corinthians 13:5). It seems appropriate that we examine ourselves in the light of God's word. We don't want to become spiritual navel-gazers, but we do want to make sure that our attitudes and actions are pleasing to him. Some people examine themselves periodically out of habit, some are prompted by the Spirit at times to look at something in their own lives, and at other times the words of a preacher or even the example of a friend may cause us to engage in a little self-examination.

After more than four decades of working with and observing ministers, I have observed that self-care is the last skill that many ministers learn. This phenomenon often occurs with spiritual leaders: They get so busy trying to help and save others that, without realizing it, they end up neglecting their own spiritual, emotional, physical, and relational health. In many cases, the full impact of such neglect does not show up for many years. I am not talking about ministers who are blatantly sinning or living a worldly lifestyle. Rather, I am referring to a minister who is becoming drained and depleted without realizing it.

It is one thing to be caring, to seek the welfare of others, and to give sacrificially of oneself—all of that is commendable. It is an entirely different thing to so neglect oneself in the process that there is nothing left to give. The former is a good thing; the latter, sadly, is negligence. If we really want to be caring and help others, one of the most important things to do is to cultivate and promote our own health and well-being so that we will be around to love and minister to others for a long time. We all need to examine ourselves in these ways also.

More attention has been given to ministers taking care of themselves in recent years, and that is a positive trend. In decades and centuries gone by, many preachers demonstrated an impressive level of consecration, but sometimes it was verbalized in terms that sounded self-destructive. For example, spiritual leaders would often say that they would "rather burn out than rust out." That may inspire some, but as many have since recognized, we don't necessarily have to do either. Both our bodies and our minds (including our emotional lives) have been given to us by God, and we should steward them well.

One of the verses that deeply impressed me when I was young and getting started in ministry was Paul's admonition to Timothy:

> **Take heed unto thyself,** *and unto the doctrine; continue in them: for in doing this thou shalt both* **save thyself,** *and them that hear thee* (1 Timothy 4:16 KJV).

I was too young to fully appreciate Paul's emphasis on Timothy taking heed to himself, but I knew there was something important being communicated. In my early twenties (which was when I began ministry), I had a sense of invincibility, as do many young people. I knew nothing about pacing myself or even the need to do such a thing.

I was excited about preaching to others and wanted to save the world. I was enamored with the work of ministry but lacked balance in my life; I had no idea why a minister would need to *"save himself"* as Paul indicated. I made important adjustments over time, and with each passing decade, I saw more and more ministers' lives implode, not because they weren't teaching and ministering well, but because they had neglected critical areas of their own personal lives.

Another translation gives Paul's words a little more clarity yet.

Give careful attention to your spiritual life and every cherished truth you teach, for living what you preach will release salvation inside you and to all those who listen to you (1 Timothy 4:16 TPT).

Here are some important applications when it comes to the art of *"taking heed unto thyself."* Each one of these is brief, but vital. This chapter is different in that Check-Up Questions follow each section instead of all being at the end of the chapter.

Take Heed to Yourself: Lifelong Growth and Development

In serving others, you can easily find yourself giving out continuously. It is necessary that you do not neglect your own personal growth and development while you are helping others. In short, you must be a lifelong learner. Remember that you are not just called to develop others, but you must also grow yourself. Paul indicated that others should be able to observe Timothy's growth and development: *"that **your progress** may be evident to all"* (1 Timothy 4:15 NKJV).

It is vital that ministers deliberately and intentionally invest in themselves. Do you make sure that your own soul is being fed? If you only study to put sermons together, it is highly unlikely that you are receiving the spiritual nutrition *you* need for *your* growth. Some of the truths that will challenge and stimulate your growth are likely beyond what you are sharing with your congregation. It is good that you provide milk to the spiritually young, but you need meat as well as milk for your own progress.

There is not just one way to cultivate your own continuing growth and development, but it is important that each one find a way that is meaningful and effective for himself or herself. In addition to good, old-fashioned Bible reading and prayer, some choose to pursue additional formal education. Others prefer informal reading and study, while others enjoy listening to podcasts and audio books or attending conferences. You may utilize different approaches to growth over the course of your ministry, but make sure that you are always taking deliberate and strategic steps toward growing yourself.

D. L. Moody was an avid learner and always sought to learn from others. His son notes that his father "was a born teacher. He was also a great learner. His capacity for drawing out information from people with whom he came in contact was marvelous."[1] He also noted, "If with a minister, he would have the best that that man could give him regarding the passages of Scripture which were especially in his mind at the time."[2]

Similarly, Moody biographer, Steve Miller, notes:

> So great was Moody's hunger for understanding the Scriptures that he eagerly took advantage of every opportunity to learn from his more knowledgeable peers. In fact, one of the reasons he desired to make his first trip to the United Kingdom was to sit and learn from gifted teachers, such as Charles Spurgeon and Andrew Bonar. Also, anytime Moody invited prominent ministers to speak at his campaigns or conferences, he would sit in the front row of the audience and listen earnestly to his guests with a notebook in hand.

> Whenever Moody found himself in the company of fellow preachers, he was sure to ask them their thoughts on certain Bible truths and passages. He felt no embarrassment in this; he saw no shame in humbly assuming the role of an inquiring student among his peers. Here is the spiritual leader as a life-long learner. Moody's attitude toward always gleaning truth from the Scriptures is one all of us should have, considering the fact the Bible contains an infinitely inexhaustible wealth of truth for us to learn.[3]

What a tremendous example to others! Moody's humility and lifelong hunger to learn is a trait that everyone who is interested in continual personal development should emulate.

As you cultivate your own spiritual development, you will ensure that you maintain vibrancy and a sense of overflow in your life. You will have living springs coming from a fresh reservoir in your own heart and mind.

The Greats Speak on Lifelong Growth and Development

Jonathan Edwards

> "Resolved, to study the Scriptures so steadily, constantly and frequently, as that I may find, and plainly perceive to grow in the knowledge of the same."

John Wesley

Howard A. Snyder writes,

> "The experience of John Wesley shows what most Christians suspect: that the essential qualifications for effective, redemptive ministry have little, if anything, to do with formal education or ecclesiastical status and everything to do with spiritual growth, maturity, and structural flexibility. On the other hand, Wesley would not long endure incompetence. He worked hard at training his helpers and traveling preachers. He practiced theological education by extension two centuries before anyone thought up the name. Preachers carried books and pamphlets for themselves and for others. They were expected constantly to 'improve the time' by up to six hours daily in study."[4]

Robert Murray McCheyne

> "The work of God would flourish by us, if it flourished more richly in us."

Richard Baxter

> "Our work must be carried on with great humility. We must carry ourselves meekly and condescendingly to all; and so teach others, as to be as ready to learn of any that can teach us, and so both teach and learn at once."

Phillips Brooks (Speaking of preparation for ministry)

> "It must be nothing less than the making of a man."

James S. Stewart

> "No man knows how to preach. You will have to reckon with this significant, disconcerting fact, that the greatest preachers who have ever lived have confessed themselves poor bunglers to the end, groping after an ideal which has eluded them forever. When you have been preaching for twenty years, you will be beginning to realize how incalculably much there is to learn."

Oswald Sanders

"A leader must be willing to develop himself on many levels and in many capacities, but with a unity of purpose."[5]

"John Wesley had a passion for reading, and he did so mostly on horseback. Often he rode a horse fifty and sometimes ninety miles in a day. His habit was to ride with a volume of science or history or medicine propped in the pommel of his saddle, and thus he consumed thousands of books."[6]

S. D. Gordon

"He can do more for others who has done most with himself."

Gordon Lindsay

"The more training a minister has, the wider an opportunity they will have to be used by God. Training one's mind promotes accuracy and preciseness of thought. It is significant that when God chose a man to write most of the epistles in the New Testament, He selected Paul—a man who had one of the best educations of his time."[7]

A. W. Tozer

> "It is especially important that Christian ministers know the law of the leader—that he can lead others only as far as he himself has gone... The minister must experience what he would teach... If he tries to bring them into a heart knowledge of truth which he has not actually experienced he will surely fail... The law of the leader tells us who are preachers that it is better to cultivate our souls than our voices."[8]

Thomas E. Trask

> "A congregation can't grow beyond the level of its leadership. If the leadership is growing, the congregation will grow proportionately in size, maturity, and development. If pastors plateau in their personal development and leadership skills, that's where their ministry will plateau."[9]

Check-Up Questions

Do you have a personal growth plan? What have you done in recent months that specifically fed your soul and helped your development? Is your intake (spiritually, emotionally, and mentally) keeping up with your outflow? What methods work best for you as you seek to cultivate continued growth? What plans do you have to feed and grow yourself over the coming months?

Take Heed to Yourself: Fervency

How is your spiritual temperature? Paul admonishes Timothy, *"I remind you to fan into flames the spiritual gift God gave you when I laid my hands on you"* (2 Timothy 1:6 NLT). You may have tended a fireplace where the embers were still glowing, but the flame had subsided. If you took the poker and stirred the embers, the flames burst forth again. Paul was not implying that Timothy's zeal had completely disappeared, but that he needed to keep his fire stirred up through the regular use of the gifts God had given him.

Every servant of God must be diligent not to neglect, quench, or extinguish the working of God's Spirit in his or her heart. Apathy, complacency, and simply "going through the motions" have no place in our lives. When Paul tells Timothy to fan the gift of God into flame, he uses a present-tense verb. In other words, he was telling Timothy to "keep fanning" your spiritual gift.[10] Great spiritual leaders through history have shared tremendous insights about staying on fire for God.

The Greats Speak on Fervency

John Wesley

> "Be zealous! Be active! Time is short!"

William Booth

> "Look well to the fire of your souls, for the tendency of fire is to go out."

Charles Spurgeon

> "Love to Jesus is the basis of all true piety, and the intensity of this love will ever be the measure of our zeal for His glory. Let us love Him with all our hearts, and then diligent labor, and consistent living will be sure to follow."

Catherine Booth

> "Be hot. God likes hot saints. Be determined that you will be hot. They will call you a fool: they did Paul. They will call you a fanatic, and say, 'This fellow is a troubler of Israel'; but you must reply, 'It is not I, but ye and your father's house, in that ye have forsaken the commandments of the Lord.' Turn the charge upon them. Hot people are never a trouble to hot people. The hotter we are the nearer we get, and the more we love one another. It is the cold people that are troubled by the hot ones. The Lord help you to be HOT."[11]

James S. Stewart

> "When all is said and done, the supreme need of the church... is men on fire for Christ."[12]

Peter Marshall

> "Enthusiasm is not contrary to reason; it is reason on fire."

Henrietta C. Mears

> "A true Christian's enthusiasm for the Lord Jesus Christ should be so exuberant that it would be far more likely to set others on fire than to be extinguished by worldly influences."

A. W. Tozer

> "God is saying, 'I stand ready to pour a little liquid fire into your heart, into your spiritual being.'"

Thomas E. Trask

> "Enthusiasm is not passion. The world has enthusiasm. The church has passion. The believer has passion. People in the world might have a form of passion, but it is really human enthusiasm. I'm talking about God-given passion. Some have erroneously equated passion with volume. But there are quiet passionate people. It is not an issue of communication style, but of sincerity and conviction."[13]

Check-Up Questions

How is the flame within you? Is it vibrant, or could it use some stirring up? What factors (perhaps now or in the past) have caused your flame to grow dim? What have you done to rekindle your flame in the past? What might you need to do now?

Take Heed to Yourself: Purity

It is disheartening every time a minister is found to have been living a double life, as it reinforces the skepticism of unbelievers and can cause the spiritually weak to stumble in their faith. Too often a person is one way in the pulpit but a very different person away from it. In the pulpit they advocated obedience to God, and yet in their private lives they walked in darkness. Not only does this bring heartache to the spouses and families of these ministers, but the principle expressed in Nathan's rebuke of David resurfaces: *"You have given great occasion to the enemies of the LORD to blaspheme..."* (2 Samuel 12:14 NKJV).

Paul understood that while ministers are human, they are still to be role models in their lifestyles. He knew that temptations would come, seeking to lure God's servants into disobedience so that the gospel they preached would be discredited in the eyes of people. As a result, he spoke strongly to Timothy about maintaining purity in his life. Here is a composite of some of these admonitions:

> *Timothy, be an example to all believers in what you say, in the way you live, in your love, your faith, and your purity* (1 Timothy 4:12 NLT).

> *Treat younger women with all purity as you would your own sisters* (1 Timothy 5:2 NLT).

> *Do not share in the sins of others. Keep yourself pure* (1 Timothy 5:22 NLT).

> *If you keep yourself pure, you will be a special utensil for honorable use. Your life will be clean, and you will be ready for the Master to use you for every good work. Run from anything that stimulates youthful lusts. Instead, pursue righteous living, faithfulness, love, and peace* (2 Timothy 2:21-22 NLT).

Paul stated that he had kept his conscience clear (2 Timothy 1:3) and encouraged Timothy to do the same (1 Timothy 1:19). He proceeded to tell Timothy that *"...some people have deliberately violated their consciences; as a result, their faith has been shipwrecked"* (1 Timothy 1:19 NLT).

The Greats Speak on Purity and Holiness

Philip Jacob Spener

> "Besides, students should unceasingly have it impressed upon them that holy life is not of less consequence than diligence and study, indeed that study without piety is worthless."[14]

John Wesley

> "The essential part of Christian holiness lies in giving your heart wholly to God."

Robert Murray McCheyne

> "Study universal holiness of life. Your whole usefulness depends on this. Your sermon on Sabbath lasts but an hour or two; your life preaches all the week. Remember, ministers are standard-bearers. Satan aims his fiery darts at them. If he can only make you a covetous minister, or a lover of pleasure, or a lover of praise, or a lover of good eating, then he has ruined your ministry forever."

Charles Spurgeon

> "It is a terrible thing when the healing balm loses its efficacy through the blunderer who administers it. You all know the injurious effects frequently produced upon water through flowing along leaden pipes; even so the gospel itself, in flowing through men who are spiritually unhealthy, may be debased until it grows injurious to their hearers."
>
> "True and genuine piety is necessary as the first indispensable requisite; whatever 'call' a man may pretend to have, if he has not been called to holiness, he certainly has not been called to the ministry."

Dwight L. Moody

> "It is a great deal better to live a holy life than to talk about it."

Oswald Sanders

> "The only safeguard for the Christian worker is, 'Holiness to the Lord' (Exodus 28:36). If we are living rightly with God, living holy lives in secret and in public, God puts a wall of fire round about us."[15]

Bruce Wilkinson

"Teachers cannot improve upon the Scriptures but they can contaminate them. A Christian who is behaving carnally clogs the communication. It's clogged in both directions—not only from the Lord but also to the people. The more Christlike our character and conduct, the clearer our message... Tragically, a divorce has occurred between the conduct and communication of many teachers. We have separated what the Lord Himself has joined together. We have said the character is not directly related to the content. What a travesty! What a mockery of the Lord... Character is God's major prerequisite for communicating His content."[16]

Check-Up Questions

The apostle James asserts it is important to *"keep oneself unspotted from the world"* (James 1:27 NKJV). How are you doing in that regard? Is there any area of compromise in your life, moral or otherwise? Are you being completely honest with yourself and with the Lord about your attitudes, thought life, and actions? Are you maintaining purity and growing in holiness?

Take Heed to Yourself: Balance

Early in ministry, before I had learned to delegate, set healthy boundaries, and pace myself, I was heavily immersed in helping others. That

is a good thing, of course, but sometimes I was not taking time to rest and to fill my own tank. One day I realized, "I am helping everyone else to have an abundant life, but my life is not feeling very abundant right now." I was drained, tired, and fatigued. My outflow (spiritually speaking) was exceeding my intake, and I was feeling the effects of it. I was taking heed to my doctrine and to serving others, but I wasn't taking heed to myself, at least not as well as I should have.

Many ministers, including me, have found out the hard way what their limits are. Some have the foresight to structure their lives and their schedules early-on in a way that is not only sustainable but enables them to thrive. Others will "hit the wall" and then hopefully make the necessary adjustments to allocate their time and energy wisely. This includes having the emotional reserves to invest richly in their most important relationships (especially spouse and children, as well as meaningful friendships) and to cultivate a rich inner life through prayer, reflection, study, play, and rest.

The Greats Speak on Balance

Augustine of Hippo

> "No man has a right to lead such a life of contemplation as to forget in his own ease the service due to his neighbor; nor has any man a right to be so immersed in active life as the neglect the contemplation of God."

Martin Luther

> "Human nature is like a drunk peasant. Lift him into the saddle on one side, over he topples on the other side."

Charles Spurgeon

> "It is not an easy thing to maintain the balance of our spiritual life. No man can be spiritually healthy who does not meditate and commune; no man, on the other hand, is as he should be unless he is active and diligent in holy service."

Check-Up Questions

Are you giving proper attention and energy to non-ministry areas of life? Are your spouse and children feeling loved and cared for? How are you doing relative to rest and play? Are you taking time to enjoy life and "smell the roses" along your journey?

Take Heed to Yourself: Health

Good health is one of our most important assets in being able to effectively fulfill our callings, but the reality is that many will face different types of health challenges throughout their ministries. It is important that we look to God as Jehovah-Rapha, the Lord who heals, but we also want to do all that we can to be good stewards of our bodies and our health.

Paul was concerned about Timothy's health, and he had reason to be. His young assistant did not seem to have the strongest constitution, and this led Paul to instruct him:

> *Don't drink only water. You ought to drink a little wine for the sake of your stomach because you are sick so often* (1 Timothy 5:23 NLT).

God had used Paul at different times to minister healing to people supernaturally, but this did not keep him from encouraging Timothy to do what he could in the natural to help himself.

Elsewhere, Paul refers to a young minister who nearly died because he overworked himself; Epaphroditus was trying to accomplish so much in serving the Lord and helping Paul (Philippians 2:25-30) that he had neglected his own health. Paul proceeds to say that God had mercy on Epaphroditus and that he had recovered. The restoration of health is a good thing, but maintaining health and precluding such calamities is even better.

Martin Luther was sickly throughout much of his adult life, and it is likely that his harsh, ascetic practices during his years as a monk contributed significantly to his ill-health. Because of his religious beliefs, Luther often abused his body as a part of his regimen of religious works. He engaged in extreme fasting and would sometimes sleep on cold floors with no blanket. Like some with a religious mindset, he thought that if he punished himself physically, it would make him more holy. Luther eventually renounced such practices, yet he lived with the consequences of the damage his body had incurred.

Robert Murray McCheyne was one of the most powerful preachers to ever grace the pulpit in Scotland; he influenced large numbers of believers at a very early age. His propensity to overwork is reflected in a statement he made shortly before his death at the age of twenty-nine: "God gave me a message to deliver and a horse to ride. Alas, I have killed the horse and now I cannot deliver the message."

Another notable and honorable minister who died at a young age was Peter Marshall, the Chaplain of the United States Senate from 1947–1949. Having pastored as well, he died of a heart attack at the age of 46. His wife, Catherine, noted his tendency toward working excessively long hours, and after his passing, she said, "In Peter's case, I am certain that it was not God's ideal will that he die of coronary occlusion at forty-six"[17]

John Wesley was a prolific writer and is most remembered for his emphasis on sanctification and holiness. Less known are Wesley's extensive efforts to help the poor and the sick. In addition to establishing dispensaries that provided rudimentary medical supplies to the poor, Wesley wrote a book entitled *Primitive Physic* which "offered the people of his day both an overall preventive approach to health and a long list of remedies for specific ailments—in all more than 800 prescriptions for more than 300 different disorders."[18]

Mark Gorveatte notes that *Primitive Physic* went through thirty-six editions and was Wesley's best-selling book.[19] Wesley was a proponent of many common-sense ideas relative to health (e.g., cleanliness, healthy eating, drinking water, vigorous exercise, adequate-but-not-excessive sleep, etc.). It appears that Wesley embraced a light form of medical work because so many could not access medical care due to their poverty, and what care was available was often not very helpful. Wesley writes:

> At length I thought of a kind of desperate expedient. "I will prepare, and give them physic myself." For six or seven and twenty years, I had made anatomy and physic the diversion of my leisure hours; though I never properly studied them, unless for a few months when I was going to America, where I imagined that I might be of some service to those who had no regular Physician among them. I applied to it again. I took into my assistance an Apothecary, and an experienced Surgeon; but to leave all difficult and complicated cases to such Physicians as the patient should choose.[20]

Through such basic care, Wesley noted that many people received help and were restored to health.

The Greats Speak on Health

Augustine

> "The Holy Spirit, too, works within, that the medicine externally applied may have some good result."

John Wesley

> "If you desire to have any health, you must never pass one day without walking, at least, an hour."[21]

Harriet Beecher Stowe

> "A woman's health is her capital."

Charles Spurgeon

> "To sit long in one posture, poring over a book, or driving a quill, is in itself a taxing of nature; but add to this a badly-ventilated chamber, a body which has long been without muscular exercise, and a heart burdened with many cares, and we have all the elements for preparing a seething cauldron of despair, especially in the dim months of fog."

Check-Up Questions

Are you being a good steward of your body? Are you getting adequate rest? Exercising? Eating well? Getting routine check-ups? Are there any changes you need to make in order to further your health and wellness?

Take Heed to Yourself: Keeping Your Soul Whole

Over the past few years, we have seen a rash of pastors taking their own lives, with some of these events getting national publicity. As tragic as each of these have been, it is important to remember that for every pastor who has actually committed suicide, thousands of others have struggled with the weight of emotional pressures and challenges.

Life and ministry sometime take an incredible toll on people. If you have not experienced that, be grateful. The book of Psalms includes numerous examples of David expressing intense emotions, such as anger, disappointment, frustration, and despair. He also found comfort and encouragement from God to make it through those times, but the struggles he went through were real.

If we look further, we find that some of the great characters of the Bible faced such crushing despair that death seemed preferable to life. For example:

- Moses told God, *"Just go ahead and kill me. Do me a favor and spare me this misery!"* (Numbers 11:15 NLT).

- Facing a great threat, Elijah *"prayed that he might die"* (1 Kings 19:4 NLT).

- In the midst of his suffering, Job wished to have never been born (Job 3:1-16) and said that he would rather die than to experience what he was going through (Job 7:15).

- Jonah was so upset at what was happening in his ministry that he told God, *"Just kill me now..."* (Jonah 4:3 NLT).

- Jeremiah also cursed the day of his birth and expressed a desire to have not been born. He said that his entire life had been *"filled with trouble, sorrow, and shame"* (Jeremiah 20:14-18 NLT).

- We get a glimpse of the pressure Paul faced while he was in the province of Asia, *"We were crushed and overwhelmed beyond our ability to endure, and we thought we would*

never live through it. In fact, we expected to die..." (2 Corinthians 1:8-9 NLT).

In a yet-to-be-published version of the New Testament—The Renner Interpretive Version—2 Corinthians 1:8-9 reads:

We would not, brethren, have you ignorant of the horribly tight, life-threatening squeeze that came to us in Asia. It was unbelievable! With all the things we've been through, this was the worst of all — it felt like our lives were being crushed. It was so difficult that I didn't know what to do. No experience I've ever been through required so much of me. In fact, I didn't have enough strength to cope with it. Toward the end of this ordeal, I was so overwhelmed that I didn't think we'd ever get out! I felt suffocated, trapped, and pinned against the wall. I really thought it was the end of the road for us! As far as we were concerned, the verdict was in, and the verdict said "death." But really, this was no great shock, because we already were feeling the effect of death and depression in our souls....[22]

I am not sharing all of this to be negative or discouraging, but to demonstrate that even some of the great spiritual leaders in the Bible went through some tremendously challenging times.

Carey Nieuhowf, who coaches and trains pastors around the world, shares his own story from 2006:

> I began to think the best way to get through this burnout was to not go through it. Because hope had died

for me in those months, I began to wonder whether that should be my preferred option as well. For the first time in my life, I began to seriously think that suicide was the best option. If I had lost hope, was no good to anyone, couldn't perform what I was expected to do, and was causing all kinds of pain to others (a conclusion that wasn't coming from a place of objectivity), then perhaps the best solution was to be no more.[23]

Nieuhowf proceeds to share several helpful insights and concludes with this heartfelt plea:

If you're married, tell your spouse, but don't *just* tell your spouse. Your pain may be too heavy a burden for your marriage alone to bear. Reach out. Please tell a friend. Tell your doctor. Tell your counsellor. Leaders, please break the silence, before the silence breaks you.[24]

You may or may not relate personally to all of this on emotional distress, but either way it may be something that will help you empathize with and help others in the future.

Many issues and challenges related to our souls will not be as intense as that of biblical leaders despairing to the point of wanting to die, and yet being self-aware and managing our emotional health is important for all of us. The book of Psalms reveals that David experienced and expressed just about every kind emotion imaginable, and he exhorts us to *"trust in him at all times. Pour out your heart to him, for God is our refuge"* (Psalm 62:8 NLT).

Jesus also experienced a wide range of emotions, as noted in the Gospels. We see him expressing joy and sorrow, as well as compassion and anger. While he continually expressed great trust in his Father, he also expressed periodic frustration with people. Likewise, a study of Paul's life reveals that he also experienced quite a spectrum of human emotions. The key to a healthy soul is not in the absence of emotions, but in the proper processing and managing of them.

This is where the uniqueness of our personalities and temperaments comes in. We are all wired differently. Some people feel things more deeply than others. Some process things internally, while others are external (or verbal) processors. Various people deal with and respond differently to different issues. You might be tempted to think that someone who processes emotions differently than you is *weird*, when in fact, they are just *wired* differently than you. What a difference the order of a couple of letters make!

Paul's admonitions reveal what may have been some of the soul challenges particularly relevant to Timothy. For example, how did Timothy, with his young age and less-than-dominating personality, handle confronting erring ministers? Paul encouraged Timothy to keep his conscience clear (1 Timothy 1:19), to avoid being intimidated (1 Timothy 4:12), to avoid impatience (1 Timothy 5:22), and to practice contentment (1 Timothy 6:6). Those are all keys to health for one's soul.

In the second epistle, Paul reminded Timothy that God had not given him *"a spirit of fear and timidity, but of power, love, and self-discipline"* and encouraged him to not be ashamed (2 Timothy 1:7-8 NLT). He later tells him to *"keep a clear mind in every situation"* and not to *"be afraid of suffering for the Lord"* (2 Timothy 4:5 NLT). Paul certainly exhorted Timothy regarding obedience, holiness, and executing his ministry, but he did not fail to show concern for the wholeness of Timothy's own soul.

The Greats Speak on Personal Wholeness

Charles Spurgeon[25]

"Do not forget the culture of the inner man—I mean of the heart. How diligently the cavalry officer keeps his sabre clean and sharp; every stain he rubs off with the greatest care. Remember you are God's sword, His instrument—I trust, a chosen vessel unto Him to bear His name. In great measure, according to the purity and perfection of the instrument, will be the success. It is not great talents God blesses so much as likeness to Jesus. A holy minister is an awful weapon in the hand of God."

"All mental work tends to weary and to depress, for much study is a weariness of the flesh; but ours is more than mental work—it is heart work, the labour of our inmost soul. How often, on Lord's-day evenings, do we feel as if life were completely washed out of us! After pouring out our souls over our congregations, we feel like empty earthen pitchers which a child might break."

"Repose is as needful to the mind as sleep to the body. Our Sabbaths are our days of toil, and if we do not rest upon some other day we shall break down. Even the

> earth must lie fallow and have her Sabbaths, and so must we."
>
> "The Master knows better than to exhaust His servants and quench the light of Israel. Rest time is not waste time. It is economy to gather fresh strength."
>
> "It is wisdom to take occasional furlough. In the long run, we shall do more by sometimes doing less."

Vance Havner

> "Satan does some of his worst work on exhausted Christians when nerves are frayed and the mind is faint."

A. W. Tozer

> "He has been made the keeper of other people's vineyards but his own vineyard has not been kept. So many demands have been made upon him that they have long ago exhausted his supply. He has been compelled to minister to others while he himself is in desperate need of a physician."[26]

Check-Up Questions

As you read this section about keeping your soul whole, did anything especially resonate with you? Were you shocked to see the many biblical characters who really struggled? Did you relate to any of those types of struggles with despair or hopelessness? Do you have trusted people in your life to whom you can turn if you face a profound challenge?

Notes

1. William R. Moody, *The Life of D. L. Moody* (Harrington, DE: Delmarva Publications, 2013), Kindle edition, 6097.

2. Ibid.

3. Steve Miller, *D. L. Moody on Spiritual Leadership* (Chicago: Moody Publishers, 2004), Kindle edition, 110-111.

4. Howard A. Snyder, *The Radical Wesley: The Patterns and Practices of a Movement Maker* (Franklin, TN: Seedbed Publishing, 2014), Kindle edition, 2529.

5. Oswald Sanders, *Dynamic Spiritual Leadership: Leading Like Paul* (Grand Rapids: Discovery House Publishers, 1999), Kindle edition, 722.

6. Oswald Sanders, *Spiritual Leadership: A Commitment to Excellence for Every Believer* (Chicago: Moody Publishers, 2007), Kindle edition, 1927.

7. Gordon Lindsay, *The Charismatic Ministry* (Dallas: Christ for the Nations, 2013), 10.

8. A. W. Tozer, "The Law of the Leader," *The Price of Neglect* (Camp Hill, PA: Wing Spread Publishers, 2010), Kindle edition, 1385-1410.

9. Thomas E. Trask, *Ministry for a Lifetime: Running the Course with Effectiveness and Endurance* (Springfield, MO: Gospel Publishing House, 2001), 90.

10. Knute Larson, *I & II Thessalonians, I & II Timothy, Titus, Philemon*, vol. 9, *Holman New Testament Commentary* (Nashville, TN: Broadman & Holman Publishers, 2000), 266. Reprinted and used by permission.

11. Catherine Booth, "Godliness," *The Catherine Booth Collection* (Christian Classic Treasury Collection, 1881), Kindle edition, 5147.

12. James S. Stewart, *Heralds of God* (Auckland, NZ: Papamoa Press, 1946), Kindle edition, 2544.

13. Thomas E. Trask, *Ministry for a Lifetime: Running the Course with Effectiveness and Endurance* (Springfield, MO: Gospel Publishing House, 2001), 74.

14. Philip Jacob Spener, *Pia Desideria* (Minneapolis: Fortress Press, 1964), Kindle edition, 1773.

15. Oswald Chambers, *Workmen of God* (Grand Rapids: Discovery House, 1993), Kindle edition, 3208.

16. Bruce Wilkinson, *The Seven Laws of the Learner: How To Teach Almost Anything to Practically Anyone* (Sisters, OR: Multnomah Publisher, 1983), 156-57.

17. Catherine Marshall, *Something More* (New York: Guideposts Edition Published by Arrangement with McGraw-Hill Co., Inc., 1974), 7.

18. *Faith & Leadership,* accessed July 16, 2021, https://faithandleadership .com/primitive-physick-john-wesley-diet-and-excercise.

19. Mark L. Gorveatte, *Lead Like Wesley: Help for Today's Ministry Servants* (Indianapolis: Wesleyan Publishing House, 2016), 13-14.

20. John Wesley, "A Plain Account of the People Called Methodists," *Wesley's Works*, Volume VIII (Grand Rapids: Baker, 1979), 264.

21. John Wesley, "Letters to Mr. Adam Clarke," *Wesley's Works*, Volume XIII (Grand Rapids: Baker, 1979), 101.

22. The RIV is an interpretive and conceptual translation of the New Testament that draws on concepts in the Greek language and interprets them in a contemporary way to provide a broader comprehension of what is being communicated through Scripture. www.renner.org.

23. Carey Nieuwhof, "Leadership and Suicide: When Ending It Seems Like the Only Way Out," accessed July, 16, 2021, https://careynieuwhof.com/leadership-and-suicide-when-ending-it-seems-like-the-only-way-out/.

24. Ibid.

25. All of these Spurgeon quotes are from his work, *Lectures to My Students*.

26. A. W. Tozer, *God Tells the Man Who Cares: God Speaks to Those Who Take Time to Listen,* Compiled by Anita M. Bailey (Chicago: Moody Publishers, 1993), Kindle edition, 104.

Chapter Five

HONOR TOWARD ALL:
*Treating People Right,
Avoiding Strife, Praying for Others*

"Honor all people. Love the brotherhood.
Fear God. Honor the king."

—1 PETER 2:17 NKJV

KEY THOUGHT: Ministry is largely a people business.
If you are going to do well serving God, you need to
get along with others and treat people well. This includes
staying out of strife and praying for people.

How to Treat Others

When Paul wrote Timothy, he gave him some very basic instructions on how he should interact with different types of people in the church:

- Older Men – *"Never speak harshly to an older man, but appeal to him respectfully as you would to your own father"* (1 Timothy 5:1 NLT).

- Younger Men – *"Talk to younger men as you would to your own brothers"* (1 Timothy 5:1 NLT).

- Older Women – *"Treat older women as you would your mother..."* (1 Timothy 5:2 NLT).

- Younger Women – *"Treat younger women with all purity as you would your own sisters"* (1 Timothy 5:2 NLT).

It is hard to over-emphasize the importance of treating people well.

After issuing the above-mentioned guidelines, Paul then spends fourteen verses giving Timothy guidelines concerning the care of widows in the church, and then he instructs him on how elders—pastors and church leaders—are to be treated, both those performing admirably and those who are not.

> *The elders who direct the affairs of the church well are worthy of double honor, especially those whose work is preaching and teaching. For Scripture says, "Do not muzzle an ox while it is treading out the grain," and "The worker deserves his wages." Do not entertain an accusation against an elder unless it is brought by two or three witnesses. But those elders who are sinning you are to reprove before everyone, so that the others may take warning. I charge you, in the sight of God and Christ Jesus and the elect angels, to keep these instructions without partiality, and to do nothing out of favoritism* (1 Timothy 5:17-21 NIV).

When Timothy is told to avoid partiality and favoritism, it reinforces Peter's admonition that all people are to be treated with honor (1 Peter 2:17).

The way we treat each other in the Body of Christ should express the love of Christ in every regard. We are to treat others with dignity and respect, not use people and coldly discard them when they are of no further use to us. Various books have been written addressing conflicts and dysfunction within churches. Some books are written about toxic and dictatorial leaders who abuse vulnerable staff and congregants. Other books are written about church members who repeatedly subvert, attack, and bring injury to pastors and their families.

True assessments as well as false accusations have been made in all directions. Some leaders have demonstrated a pattern of overbearing, degrading behaviors toward others, but the majority of church leaders are good, caring individuals who truly want to help people mature in their faith. It is not fair to paint them with the same brush as the ones who have caused much injury. Likewise, some church members repeatedly cause pain and chaos in the lives of pastors, but the majority of church members are not that way and desire good for their spiritual leaders.

Before you think about giving up on the church, just remember that wherever there are people, there will be problems. We are called to be problem-solvers and peacemakers. As long as humans have been on the earth, conflicts have existed between them. Sadly, the church is not exempt. Paul addressed the Corinthian church, saying, *"...You are jealous of one another and quarrel with each other..."* (1 Corinthians 3:3 NLT). He also told two leaders in the church in Philippi to settle their disagreement (Philippians 4:2). The apostle James addressed *"quarrels and fights"* that were taking place among the believers he wrote to (James 4:1 NLT). These are all sad, but as J. C. Ryle said, "Before Christ comes it is useless to expect to see a perfect Church."

Handling Contention and Contentious People

As important as Paul's instructions were about relating to other people, perhaps he gave the most attention to warning Timothy about foolish and unprofitable controversies. No doubt, he wanted Timothy to focus on the essentials and not get bogged down in minutiae. This makes me wonder how much more Paul might have stressed this same topic had he been able to witness the countless, unprofitable theological skirmishes that take place on social media in the twenty-first century. Even so, Paul gave very strong directives along these lines in the first century. He spoke of:

- Those who have *"an unhealthy desire to quibble over the meaning of words"* as *"this stirs up arguments ending in jealousy, division, slander, and evil suspicions"* (1 Timothy 6:4 NLT).

- *"Godless, foolish discussions"* (1 Timothy 6:20 NLT).

- *"Stop fighting over words"* and *"such arguments are useless"* (2 Timothy 2:14 NLT).

- *"Avoid worthless, foolish talk"* (2 Timothy 2:16 NLT).

- *"Don't get involved in foolish, ignorant arguments that only start fights,"* and, *"A servant of the Lord must not quarrel"* (2 Timothy 2:23-24 NLT).

It is one thing to be friendly to others; that is a good thing. It is another thing entirely to be able to lead people well. Ministers soon learn that some have agendas that do not promote the best interests of the church, and navigating such situations requires wisdom and strength, as well as patience and diplomacy. Timothy had learned from Paul that people have different needs, and there are guidelines for dealing with various types of people. For example, Paul had admonished the church in Thessalonica to *"warn those who are idle and disruptive, encourage the disheartened, help the weak, be patient with everyone"* (1 Thessalonians 5:14 NIV).

Paul recognized that not all people could be treated the same, but he wanted his young associates to be as kind as they could be, while being as firm as they needed to be. Because of the dangers of false teaching, he had admonished Timothy's counterpart, Titus, that *"if people are causing divisions among you, give a first and second warning. After that, have nothing more to do with them"* (Titus 3:10 NLT). Further, Paul had warned the church at Rome:

> *Watch out for people who cause divisions and upset people's faith by teaching things contrary to what you have been taught. Stay away from them. Such people are not serving Christ our Lord; they are serving their own personal interests. By smooth talk and glowing words they deceive innocent people* (Romans 16:17-18 NLT).

Spiritual leaders must have significant levels of discernment, courage, and resolve.

When all of this is considered, ministers have to cover a wide range of territory in their dealings with people, and all of this must be done representing the Lord Jesus Christ.

Insights from History

Martin Luther, who fought more spiritual battles than any of us could imagine, stated, "A preacher must be both soldier and shepherd. He must nourish, defend, and teach; he must have teeth in his mouth, and be able to bite and fight." While there is some hyperbole in Luther's words, the principle he conveys is valid. Ministers should not be run over by bullies, but neither should they become bullies toward others. Preachers should care for the flock and be willing to confront wolves. Likewise, congregants should be supportive and honoring toward their leaders.

Perhaps the most famous hymn ever written is "Amazing Grace," penned by the former slave trader, John Newton (1725–1807). Painfully aware of his own sinful past and thankful for how merciful God had been toward him, Newton encouraged Christians to maintain a humble and gracious spirit in controversies and disagreements with others. Especially in doctrinal disputes, Newton encouraged believers to be loving and prayerful toward "opponents" and to avoid developing a haughty, contentious attitude.

> I wish that before you set pen to paper against him, and during the whole time you are preparing your answer, you may commend him by earnest prayer to the Lord's teaching and blessing. The Lord loves him and bears with him; therefore you must not despise him, or treat him harshly. The Lord bears with you likewise, and expects that you should show tenderness to others, from a sense of the much forgiveness you need yourself. In a little while you will meet in heaven; he will then be dearer to you than the nearest friend

> you have upon earth is to you now. Anticipate that
> period in your thoughts; and though you may find it
> necessary to oppose his errors, view him personally
> as a kindred soul, with whom you are to be happy in
> Christ forever.[1]

Newton continues:

> What will it profit a man if he gains his cause and
> silences his adversary, if at the same time he loses that
> humble, tender frame of spirit in which the Lord
> delights, and to which the promise of his presence is
> made? If we act in a wrong spirit, we shall bring little
> glory to God, do little good to our fellow creatures,
> and procure neither honor nor comfort to ourselves.
> If you can be content with showing your wit, and gain-
> ing the laugh on your side, you have an easy task; but
> I hope you have a far nobler aim, and that, sensible of
> the solemn importance of gospel truths, and the com-
> passion due to the souls of men...[2]

Long before John Newton made his appeals for kindness and
compassion toward those espousing differing views, Philip Spener
(1635–1705) stated that "we must beware how we conduct ourselves
in religious controversies with unbelievers and heretics."[3] Concerning
the erring, he reminds believers to pray for those that are deemed to
be off track and to avoid unnecessarily offending them. Though he
states that truth should be communicated firmly, we must maintain "a
heartfelt love toward them."[4]

Spener speaks of how distasteful disputes had become in his day and challenged believers to avoid personal insults and any attitudes that would work against restoring an erring brother. He states that "we should demonstrate that we consider these people to be our neighbors"[5] and that "A proper hatred of false religion should neither suspend nor weaken the love that is due the other person."[6] Finally, he asserts that "disputing is not enough either to maintain the truth among ourselves or to impart it to the erring. The holy love of God is necessary."[7]

Today, we can appreciate these encouragements in the light of scathing articles and harsh social media posts that are sometimes made by Christians against other believers with whom they disagree. However, in Spener's day and in previous generations, there were far worse expressions of hostility shown toward theological opponents. While we respect many of Martin Luther's theological insights and his work in launching the Reformation, it is hard to not grimace at the brutal name-calling and vulgar insults he often hurled at his adversaries. One hundred years before Luther, an earlier Reformer named Jan Hus had been burned at the stake by religious opponents for his beliefs. Later, William Tyndale would face a similar fate (though he was strangled first) for having translated the New Testament into English and teaching doctrine contrary to the established church.

Anabaptists (those who rejected infant baptism in favor of adult baptism upon a profession of faith) were harshly persecuted throughout Europe, and some of their leaders were even drowned in Zurich a short distance from Ulrich Zwingli's church. In Calvin's Geneva, heresy was punishable by death, and Calvin's legacy has been tarnished by his approval of the execution of one of his theological opponents, Michael Servetus, in 1553.

As we consider the history of how different ones have handled conflict and controversy through church history, we should remember the commandment that Jesus gave, that we are to even love our enemies and to pray for those who persecute us (Matthew 5:44). Jesus commended the church of Ephesus because they stood for truth, but he rebuked them because they were failing in their love walk (Revelation 2:4).

As much as Paul wanted Timothy to be committed to the truth, he did not want him becoming bitter and hateful toward those who held differing views. He admonished him:

> *A servant of the Lord must not quarrel but must be **kind** to everyone, be able to teach, and be **patient** with difficult people. **Gently** instruct those who oppose the truth. Perhaps God will change those people's hearts, and they will learn the truth. Then they will come to their senses and escape from the devil's trap. For they have been held captive by him to do whatever he wants* (2 Timothy 2:24-26 NLT).

Three elements that Paul wanted Timothy to possess when dealing with conflict were kindness, patience, and gentleness. May all of God's ministers possess these yet today.

Putting Others to Work

I occasionally hear ministers speak of how difficult it is to get others involved in serving and taking responsibility, and I empathize with that. Regardless, one of the greatest responsibilities (and privileges) of serving God involves enlisting and training others and then releasing them into their own fruitful and productive ministry for the Lord. Paul admonishes Timothy:

You have heard me teach things that have been confirmed by many reliable witnesses. Now teach these truths to other trustworthy people who will be able to pass them on to others (2 Timothy 2:2 NLT).

Timothy himself had been recognized and recruited by Paul and then put to work after being trained and mentored. Oswald Sanders notes:

> Paul assigned Timothy tasks far above his conscious ability, but encouraged and fortified him in their execution. How else could a young man develop his powers and capacities than by tackling situations that extend him to the limit?[8]

Paul was asking Timothy, then, to recruit, train, and activate others just as he had done for him.

John Wesley was known as a great organizer, and this included organizing people for discipleship purposes and mobilizing people for service. Whitefield was a great preacher—most felt he was better and more dynamic than Wesley. However, Whitefield lacked Wesley's organizational genius and said of his peer:

> My brother Wesley acted wisely. The souls that were awakened under his ministry he joined in class and thus preserved the fruits of his labours. This I neglected, and my people are a rope of sand.[9]

At one point, Wesley and his leaders became aware of the massive health crisis that many in London were facing. Always the strategist, Wesley describes what happened as he met with his leaders about this problem:

> The next morning many willingly offered themselves. I chose six-and-forty of them, whom I judged to be the most tender, loving spirit; divided the town into twenty-three parts, and desired two of them to visit the sick in each division.[10]

Wesley gave these workers basic instructions and dispatched them to visit the sick and minister to them three times a week.

In addition to the dispensing of basic medical care described in the previous chapter, Wesley and his workers also provided spiritual ministry and prayer for the sick. In his journal, Wesley later wrote that this work continued for several years and stated, "Through the blessing of God, many who had been ill for months or years, were restored to perfect health."[11] Through delegation, Wesley was implementing most successfully what Jesus had advocated centuries before:

> *He said to his disciples, "The harvest is great, but the workers are few. So pray to the Lord who is in charge of the harvest; ask him to send more workers into his fields"* (Matthew 9:37-38 NLT).

Delegation is not just dumping excessive or unwanted details on someone else. Rather, delegation begins with recognizing that God has called many people into his harvest field and that it takes far more than just one person to accomplish the task.

D. L. Moody was another great mobilizer of the saints. He once said that he would rather put a thousand men to work than to do the work of a thousand men. Moody also said, "If this world is going to be reached, I am convinced it must be done by men and women of average talent. After all there are comparatively few people in the world who have great talents."[12] Biographer Steve Miller writes:

> Moody believed that all Christians have a place of service to the Lord—not just leaders. He relied heavily on the help of "average" Christians in his evangelistic meetings everywhere. He saw the masses of believers in the pews as a tremendous source of untapped power— as armies who could help advance Christ's kingdom even if ministry never became their occupation.[13]

Further Insights

Oswald Sanders spoke of training and mobilizing others in the following terms:

> Christians everywhere have undiscovered and unused spiritual gifts. The leader must help bring those gifts into the service of the kingdom, to develop them, to marshal their power.[14]
>
> The promising convert should be given a widening opportunity to serve at humbler and less prominent tasks that will develop both natural and spiritual gifts.

He should not be advanced too fast, lest he become puffed up. Neither should he be repressed, lest he become discouraged.[15]

Churches grow in every way when they are guided by strong, spiritual leaders with the touch of the supernatural radiating in their service. The church sinks into confusion and malaise without such leadership. Today those who preach with majesty and spiritual power are few, and the booming voice of the church has become a pathetic whisper. Leaders today—those who are truly spiritual—must take to heart their responsibility to pass on the torch to younger people as a firstline duty.[16]

Pentecostal leader, Donald Gee writes:

No shepherd can have much to do with the sheep under his care without generally coming to see that some are more fitted for certain work than others. Any shepherd worthy of the name studies his flock. Some are plainly able to speak in public, whilst others (equally precious children of God) have no gifts at all that way. Some are good with children, others not. Some have business ability, some have none. Some have a winsome way, and are quickly at home with strangers, others are the very reverse. All these things are to be noted, for God usually works along the line of our natural makeup, even when He also gives spiritual gifts.[17]

Gee proceeds:

> There must be opportunity. This is where some excellent pastors fail. They keep everything too tightly in their own hands. Quite probably their larger experience in Christian work may enable them to do some things a little more competently than other folk; but that is no reason why they should "do" everything. From one aspect it is a serious form of selfishness. Such a policy produces a barren Assembly—as far as workers are concerned. Ultimately the boomerang returns upon the pastors' own head; he becomes crushed with the work which could have been shared by others, and narrowly escapes a breakdown. It is loss from every point of view. Give opportunity.[18]

Praying for Leaders and for All People

One cannot read Paul's letters without realizing how essential prayer was in his life. He knew that ministry was not something he did in his own ability and strength; Paul was continually mindful that all he did was in concert and partnership with God. As a result, we see him regularly praying for his readers and speaking words of blessing over them—even requesting prayer for himself.

When Paul wrote Timothy, he admonished him to make prayer a primary and integral part of his life and ministry and to make it central in the life of the church as well.

I urge you, first of all, to pray for all people. Ask God to help them; intercede on their behalf, and give thanks for them. Pray this way for kings and all who are in authority so that we can live peaceful and quiet lives marked by godliness and dignity. This is good and pleases God our Savior, who wants everyone to be saved and to understand the truth.... In every place of worship, I want men to pray with holy hands lifted up to God, free from anger and controversy (1 Timothy 2:1-4, 8 NLT).

These prayers, intercessions, and giving of thanks were initially directed toward *"all people,"* but then Paul specifies the inclusion of *"kings and all who are in authority."*

No doubt many have found praying *for* earthly rulers to be challenging, as there has been no shortage of corrupt leaders throughout history, with numbers of them opposing the people and the work of God. Perhaps no one personified the grace to pray more than William Tyndale (1494–1536). Tyndale's translation of the New Testament into the English language drew the wrath of both secular and religious officials. Before Tyndale was strangled to death and his body burnt at the stake, his final words were, "Lord, open the King of England's eyes!"

Concerning Paul's admonition to Timothy, Rick Renner writes, "If anyone needed prayer, it was the unsaved kings who possessed lofty positions of power and authority in the First Century AD!"[19] Renner continues:

> Most believers in New Testament times had no option
> to vote, so they did what they could do... I'm sure if

> they had been given the right to vote, they would have rushed to the polling booths to cast their votes. But the only vote they could cast was in prayer — so they prayed! Since their governmental leaders were entrenched in power and there was nothing they could do to change it, these early believers took their role in prayer very seriously.[20]

This is a great reminder that none of our political views or preferences negate God's word, which teaches us that we are to pray for all people, including those in authority.

Along these same lines, it is important to remember Jesus' very clear directives:

> *You have heard the law that says, "Love your neighbor" and hate your enemy. But I say, love your enemies! Pray for those who persecute you! In that way, you will be acting as true children of your Father in heaven. For he gives his sunlight to both the evil and the good, and he sends rain on the just and the unjust alike. If you love only those who love you, what reward is there for that? Even corrupt tax collectors do that much. If you are kind only to your friends, how are you different from anyone else? Even pagans do that. But you are to be perfect, even as your Father in heaven is perfect* (Matthew 5:43-48 NLT).

Perhaps we have read that so many times that we fail to absorb the meaning and impact that Jesus intended for it to have. Try putting yourself into the shoes of those who first heard these words. In addition to whatever *personal* enemies the different individuals might

have had, Jesus was speaking to Jewish people who had known many enemies on a *national* level.

They had been held captive by the Egyptians, Assyrians, and Babylonians, and they were currently under Roman occupation and oppression. They had struggled against Canaanites, Amalekites, Edomites, Moabites, Syrians, Ammonites, Midianites, and Philistines, just to name a few. The Israelites had struggled for survival for so long, and now Jesus comes along and tells them, *"Love your enemies! Pray for those who persecute you!"*

Paul refers to one of his fellow-workers named Clement (Philippians 4:3). It is unknown if this is the same individual who later became a Bishop in the Empire's capital city, but Clement of Rome prayed the following for *"our rulers and governors upon the earth."*

> You, Master, have given the power of the kingdom to them through your magnificent and indescribable power, so that we may know the glory and honor given to them by you, and be subject to them, in no way opposing your will. To whom, Lord, give health, peace, harmony, and good disposition so that they may administer the government given by you to them without stumbling. For you, heavenly Master, King of the ages, have given to the sons of men glory and honor and power over the things which belong upon the earth. You, Lord, direct their plan according to what is good and pleasing in your presence, so that, piously administering with peace and gentleness, the authority given by you to them, they may experience your mercy. The only one able to do these things and even better things for us, to you we give praise through

> the high priest and defender of our souls, Jesus Christ, through whom be glory and majesty to you, both now and for all generations and forever, amen.[21]

Incidentally, at the time Clement wrote this prayer, Domitian—the emperor who exiled John to Patmos—was ruling as the emperor.

Clement's prayer is a dynamic reminder that we are not just to pray for leaders because we appreciate their politics or agree with their policies. In the midst of Paul's admonition for Timothy to pray is a vital truth that should govern all we do, that God *desires all men to be saved and to come to the knowledge of the truth"* (1 Timothy 2:4 NKJV). Never forget and never underestimate the power of prayer!

Richard Halverson, who served as the Chaplain of the United States Senate for fourteen years said:

> Intercession is truly universal work for the Christian. No place is closed to intercessory prayer. No continent—no nation—no organization—no city—no office. There is no power on earth that can keep intercession out.

May a generation of believers arise who will take the call to prayer seriously, and may all that we do be saturated with God's very presence. Prayer not only brings us into alignment with God, but it also enables us to partner with him as he carries out his will in the earth.

The Greats Speak on Giving Honor and Treating People Right

Augustine of Hippo

> "You have enemies. For who can live on this earth without them? Take heed to yourselves: love them. In no way can your enemy so hurt you by his violence, as you hurt yourself if you love him not."

Thomas A' Kempis

> "Try to bear patiently with the defects and infirmities of others, whatever they may be, because you also have many a fault which others must endure. If you cannot make yourself what you would wish to be, how can you bend others to your will? We want them to be perfect, yet we do not correct our own faults."

Johannes Oecolampadius (Protestant Reformer writing to William Farel)

> "Your mission is to evangelize, not to curse. Prove yourself to be an evangelist, not a tyrannical legislator. Men want to be led, not driven."

John Wesley

> "Your temper is uneven; you lack love for your neighbors. You grow angry too easily; your tongue is too sharp—thus the people will not hear you." (Wesley writing to a preacher)
>
> "See that you are courteous toward all men. It matters not, in this respect, whether they are high or low, rich or poor, superior or inferior to you. No, not even whether good or bad, whether they fear God or not. Indeed, the mode of showing your courtesy may vary, as Christian prudence will direct; but the thing itself is due to all; the lowest and the worst have a claim to our courtesy."
>
> "Though we cannot think alike, may we not love alike? May we not be of one heart, though we are not of one opinion?"

George Washington Carver

> "How far you go in life depends on your being tender with the young, compassionate with the aged, sympathetic with the striving and tolerant of the weak and strong. Because someday in your life you will have been all of these."

Dietrich Bonhoeffer

"The Christian must treat his enemy as a brother, and requite his hostility with love. His behavior must be determined not by the way others treat him, but by the treatment he himself receives from Jesus; it has only one source, and that is the will of Jesus."[22]

"I can no longer condemn or hate a brother for whom I pray, no matter how much trouble he causes me."[23]

Gordon Lindsay

"There are many things that can cause ministers to fail. Among them are laziness, incompetency, and ineffectiveness in the pulpit. But one of the great causes of failure is the minister's lack of kindness or tact."[24]

"There are some leaders who might strive to reach a high position in God's eyes, except that they insist on using people for their own advancement. We all need one another. Without the assistance of others, the greatest among us would not go far. The least a leader can show to those who have helped him is gratitude. Unfortunately, there are those who use others to further their own interests, and then, ruthlessly set them aside without a second thought."[25]

Warren Wiersbe

"A leader shows the church what to do by example; the dictator tells the church what to do. A leader depends on humility, prayer, and love; a dictator depends on pressure, force, and fear. The true leader goes before and encourages; the dictator stands behind and drives. The leader leads by serving; the dictator expects others to serve him. The leader rejoices when God gets the glory and others get the credit; the dictator takes both the credit and the glory for himself. The leader builds people; the dictator uses people and then drops them when he is through exploiting them."[26]

Oswald Sanders

"If you would rather pick a fight than solve a problem, do not consider leading the church. The Christian leader must be genial and gentle, not a lover of controversy."[27]

C. Gene Wilkes

"People prefer to follow those who help them, not those who intimidate them."[28]

John Stott

"The authority by which the Christian leader leads is not power but love, not force but example, not coercion but reasoned persuasion. Leaders have power, but power is safe only in the hands of those who humble themselves to serve."

Check-Up Questions

Do you believe you treat all people respectfully? What does not showing favoritism mean to you? Do you steer clear of strife and unnecessary controversies? Do you maintain your peace and your love walk when people are in opposition? Do you pray for leaders even if you disagree with their policies?

Notes

1. John Newton, "A Guide to Godly Disputation," *The Letters of John Newton* (Tigard, OR: Monergism Books, 2010), Kindle edition, 398.

2. Ibid., 472.

3. Philip Jacob Spener, *Pia Desideria* (Minneapolis: Fortress Press, 1964), Kindle edition, 1664.

4. Ibid., 1678.

5. Ibid., 1688.

6. Ibid., 1693.

7. Ibid., 1738.

8. Oswald Sanders, *Dynamic Spiritual Leadership: Leading Like Paul* (Grand Rapids: Discovery House Publishers, 1999), Kindle edition, 3361.

9. John Pollock, *George Whitefield: The Evangelist* (Scotland: Christian Focus Publications, 1973), Kindle edition, 3134.

10. John Wesley, "A Plain Account of the People Called Methodists," *The Works of John Wesley*, Third Edition, Volume VIII (Grand Rapids, Baker Book House, 1978), 263.

11. John Wesley, "Journal," *The Works of John Wesley*, Third Edition, Volume II (Grand Rapids, Baker Book House, 1978), December 4, 1746, 39.

12. William R. Moody, *Life of D. L. Moody* (Chicago: Revell, 1990), 87.

13. Steve Miller, *D. L. Moody on Spiritual Leadership* (Chicago: Moody Publishers, 2004), Kindle edition, 12.

14. Oswald Sanders, *Spiritual Leadership: A Commitment to Excellence for Every Believer* (Chicago: Moody Publishers, 2007), Kindle edition, 1555.

15. Ibid., 838.

16. Ibid., 318.

17. Donald Gee, *Concerning Shepherds and Sheepfolds: A Series of Studies Dealing with Shepherds and Sheepfolds* (London: Elim Publishing Company, 1952), 67-68.

18. Ibid., 68-69.

19. Rick Renner, "Praying for Those in Authority," *Sparkling Gems from the Greek,* Vol. II (Shippensburg, PA: Harrison House, 2016), 614. Copyright © 2003 by Rick Renner. All rights reserved. Used by permission of Destiny Image Publishers., Shippensburg PA, 17257.

20. Ibid., 615.

21. Rick Brannan, translator, *The Apostolic Fathers in English* (Bellingham, WA: Lexham Press, 2012).

22. Dietrich Bonhoeffer, *The Cost of Discipleship* (New York: Touchstone, 2012), Kindle edition, 148.

23. Dietrich Bonhoeffer, *Life Together: The Classic Exploration of Christian Community* (London: SCM Press, 1954), Kindle edition, 50.

24. Gordon Lindsay, *The Charismatic Ministry* (Dallas: Christ for the Nations, 2013), 24.

25. Ibid., 169-170.

26. Warren Wiersbe, *Listening to the Giants* (Grand Rapids: Baker, 1980), 352.

27. Oswald Sanders, *Spiritual Leadership: A Commitment to Excellence for Every Believer* (Chicago: Moody Publishers, 2007), Kindle edition, 838.

28. Lynn Anderson, *They Smell Like Sheep: Spiritual Leadership for the 21st Century* (West Monroe, LA: Howard Publishing, 1997), 58.

Chapter Six

UNSHAKABLE AND UNMOVABLE:

Being Grounded in Truth

"Truth is mighty and will prevail."

—*Thomas Brooks*

KEY THOUGHT: The world needs truth that is clear, compelling, and convicting. When it comes to the essentials of the gospel, we do not need fuzzy, vague, and obtuse ideas about a general concept of God. We need absolute clarity about the God and Father of our Lord Jesus Christ and all that his plan of redemption involves.

People typically think of Paul's communications to Timothy as very practical letters encouraging a young pastor with instructions on how to carry out his ministerial responsibilities. While that assessment is correct, it is not complete. One should not fail to recognize that Paul's letters to Timothy are also richly laden with doctrinal truth. Gospel truth—divinely revealed truth—must be at the core of every minister's identity and calling.

While encouraging people is good, God's ministers are not merely called to be motivational speakers. We are not self-help gurus who occasionally mention Jesus. Rather, we are entrusted with eternal truth and an everlasting gospel, and like Aaron, we stand between the living and the dead (Numbers 16:48).

Paul's letters to Timothy were not written as a generic Pastor's Manual, although they contain many vital principles for all spiritual leaders. A significant part of what Paul wrote was *occasional*. By that, I mean that Paul was addressing precise issues that were happening in that specific locale, at that specific time in history, and in that particular culture. The reader must be able to delineate specifics Paul was addressing as opposed to what ministers might be facing today.

For example, the doctrinal errors encountered by ministers today could be quite different than those Timothy was having to address. Today's pastor might not have to address the false idea of the resurrection having already taken place (2 Timothy 2:18), but the idea of confronting false teaching is a transcendent principle that applies today. Also, none of us are being asked to get Paul's coat and books and take them to him (2 Timothy 4:13), but the principle of serving others in need remains an important practice.

We live in a day of extreme relativism. Many reject the idea of absolute truth and, instead, promote the idea that everyone has their own personal truth. Paul, though, states that *"God's truth stands firm like a foundation stone..."* (2 Timothy 2:19 NLT). Jesus said, *"I am the way, the truth, and the life. No one can come to the Father except through me"* (John 14:6 NLT). Unfortunately, things have not changed a lot since Paul preached in Athens to people who *"spent their time doing nothing but talking about and listening to the latest ideas"* (Acts 17:21 NIV).

Our world is swimming in an ocean of isms (atheism, secular humanism, moral relativism, universalism, antinomianism, etc.) that

are in stark opposition to the truth of God's word. If there is no such thing as absolute truth, then ministers have no right to declare, "Thus says the Lord." However, if there is absolute truth, then we have a vital responsibility to do everything within our power to make his word known, so that we can share in the same type of gospel proclamation in which Paul engaged:

> *...to open their eyes, so they may turn from darkness to light and from the power of Satan to God. Then they will receive forgiveness for their sins and be given a place among God's people, who are set apart by faith in me* (Acts 26:18 NLT).

Truth really does matter, both ultimately and eternally.

Occasionally, you may hear people disparage the importance of doctrine and theology. I have heard people make statements to the effect that "we don't want any doctrine or theology around here." I am sure (or at least I hope) that such individuals were actually referring to human traditions that are contrary to the truth of God's word. We must realize that doctrine is not a bad thing; what is bad is bad doctrine. Likewise, theology is not a bad thing; what is bad is bad theology.

Instilling doctrine into the lives of believers was one of Paul's top priorities for Timothy. He admonished his young protégé, *"Till I come, give attention to reading, to exhortation, to doctrine"* (1 Timothy 4:13 NKJV). *Doctrine* simply refers to what is taught, and every true minister of the gospel wants the truth to be taught. *Theology* refers to the knowledge of God, and all true ministers desire that God, in all of his goodness and mercy, be accurately presented to people so that they receive salvation and truly come to know him.

As Paul coached Timothy, he repeatedly reminded him of the basics—the ABCs of the Christian faith. I feel confident that Paul had talked to Timothy about doctrinal and theological matters in-depth in their private conversations and that Timothy had also heard Paul teach such truths in various settings. I believe that, in his letters, Paul was simply reminding Timothy about teachings he had shared with him many times before. Here are some of the key doctrinal elements Paul reiterated to Timothy.

Soteriology (The Doctrine of Salvation)

"Christ Jesus came into the world to save sinners" (1 Timothy 1:15 NLT).

"God our Savior... wants all people to be saved and to come to the knowledge of the truth" (1 Timothy 2:3-4 NASB).

"Our hope is in the living God, who is the Savior of all people and particularly of all believers" (1 Timothy 4:10 NLT).

"He [Jesus] gave his life to purchase freedom for everyone" (1 Timothy 2:6 NLT).

"God saved us and called us to live a holy life. He did this, not because we deserved it, but because that was his plan from before the beginning of time—to show us his grace through Christ Jesus" (2 Timothy 1:9 NLT).

Hamartiology (The Doctrine of Sin)

"...'Christ Jesus came into the world to save sinners'—and I am the worst of them all. But God had mercy on me so that Christ Jesus could use me as a prime example of his great patience with even the worst sinners. Then others will realize that they, too, can believe in him and receive eternal life" (1 Timothy 1:15-16 NLT).

Paul's instructions to Timothy on salvation include his reference to the purpose of the law, which was to reveal sin. As Paul taught extensively in Romans and Galatians, the law was never given to save people, but to show them their need for salvation. Grace brings righteousness, but the law reveals human sinfulness so that we will know we need a Savior. As a result, Paul reminds Timothy:

"We know that the law is good when used correctly. For the law was not intended for people who do what is right. It is for people who are lawless and rebellious, who are ungodly and sinful, who consider nothing sacred and defile what is holy, who kill their father or mother or commit other murders. The law is for people who are sexually immoral, or who practice homosexuality, or are slave traders, liars, promise breakers, or who do anything else that contradicts the wholesome teaching that comes from the glorious Good News entrusted to me by our blessed God" (1 Timothy 1:8-11 NLT).

In addition, Paul refers to insolence, violations of conscience, blasphemy, anger and controversy, heavy drinking, violence, quarreling,

covetousness, pride, dishonesty with money, slander, hypocrisy and lying, arguing, laziness, gossip, meddling in the business of others, favoritism, being disrespectful, jealousy, division, slander and evil suspicions, the love of money, craving money, foolish talk, godless behavior, evil and youthful lusts, being self-absorbed, boasting, scoffing at God, disobedience to parents, ungratefulness, not loving, unforgiveness, uncontrolled, cruel, hating good, betrayal, recklessness, loving pleasure rather than God, and deception (1 Timothy 1:13, 19-20; 2:8; 3:3, 6, 8, 11; 4:2, 7; 5:13, 21; 6:2, 4, 10; 2 Timothy 2:16, 19, 22; 3:2-4, 13).

> *"Remember, the sins of some people are obvious, leading them to certain judgment. But there are others whose sins will not be revealed until later"* (1 Timothy 5:24 NLT).

Theology (The Doctrine of God)

> *"All honor and glory to God forever and ever! He is the eternal King, the unseen one who never dies; he alone is God. Amen"* (1 Timothy 1:17 NLT).

> *"...God our Savior, who wants everyone to be saved and to understand the truth. For, there is one God..."* (1 Timothy 2:3-5 NLT).

> *"Everything God created is good..."* (1 Timothy 4:4 NLT).

> *"...God, who gives life to all..."* (1 Timothy 6:13 NLT).

> *"He alone can never die, and he lives in light so brilliant that no human can approach him. No human eye has ever seen him, nor ever will. All honor and power to him forever! Amen"* (1 Timothy 6:16 NLT).

Ecclesiology (The Doctrine of the Church)

Paul describes how he wants men to pray *"in every place of worship"* (1 Timothy 2:8 NLT).

Paul refers to *"the household of God"* and writes, *"This is the church of the living God, which is the pillar and foundation of the truth"* (1 Timothy 3:15 NLT). He spent fourteen verses prior to this (1 Timothy 3:1-14) articulating the spiritual requirements for church leaders.

In 1 Timothy 5:3-16, Paul gives detailed instructions on how the church at Ephesus was to care for widows, and in 1 Timothy 5:17-22, he presents additional guidelines relative to church leaders—compensation, discipline, and ordination.

Christology (The Doctrine of Christ)

> *"There is one God and one Mediator who can reconcile God and humanity—the man Christ Jesus. He gave his life to purchase freedom for everyone..."* (1 Timothy 2:5-6 NLT).

"Without question, this is the great mystery of our faith: Christ was revealed in a human body and vindicated by the Spirit. He was seen by angels and announced to the nations. He was believed in throughout the world and taken to heaven in glory" (1 Timothy 3:16 NLT).

"...Christ Jesus, who gave a good testimony before Pontius Pilate" (1 Timothy 6:13 NLT).

"...Christ Jesus, our Savior... broke the power of death and illuminated the way to life and immortality through the Good News" (2 Timothy 1:10 NLT).

"Always remember that Jesus Christ, a descendant from King David, was raised from the dead..." (2 Timothy 2:8 NLT).

Pneumatology (the Doctrine of the Holy Spirit)

"...the power of the Holy Spirit who lives within us..." (2 Timothy 1:14 NLT).

"Now the Holy Spirit tells us clearly..." (1 Timothy 4:1 NLT).

Bibliology (The Doctrine of Scripture)

> *"...the word of truth"* (2 Timothy 2:15 NLT).

> *"You have been taught the holy Scriptures from childhood, and they have given you the wisdom to receive the salvation that comes by trusting in Christ Jesus. All Scripture is inspired by God and is useful to teach us what is true and to make us realize what is wrong in our lives. It corrects us when we are wrong and teaches us to do what is right. God uses it to prepare and equip his people to do every good work"* (2 Timothy 3:15-17 NLT).

Eschatology (The Doctrine of Last Things)

Paul censured the erroneous teaching of those who were purporting, *"the resurrection of the dead has already occurred"* (2 Timothy 2:18 NLT).

> *"...in the last times some will turn away from the true faith; they will follow deceptive spirits and teachings that come from demons"* (1 Timothy 4:1 NLT).

> *"...until our Lord Jesus Christ comes again. For, at just the right time Christ will be revealed from heaven..."* (1 Timothy 6:14-15 NLT).

"...they will be storing up their treasure as a good foundation for the future so that they may experience true life" (1 Timothy 6:19 NLT).

"...the day of Christ's return" (2 Timothy 1:18 NLT).

"...in the last days there will be very difficult times" (2 Timothy 3:1 NLT).

"I solemnly urge you in the presence of God and Christ Jesus, who will someday judge the living and the dead when he comes to set up his Kingdom" (2 Timothy 4:1 NLT).

"And now the prize awaits me—the crown of righteousness, which the Lord, the righteous Judge, will give me on the day of his return. And the prize is not just for me but for all who eagerly look forward to his appearing" (2 Timothy 4:8 NLT).

Paul wanted Timothy to be solidly grounded in revealed truth. What difference would it make if Timothy was a confident and secure leader but could not clearly articulate truth? What would the benefit be if Timothy had mastered all kinds of managerial and leadership skills and was a clever communicator, but did not have divine truth at the core of his own heart and at the center of his messages?

Timothy was not simply a motivational speaker or the head of a social club. Rather, he was charged with a most solemn responsibility—that of watching over souls and sharing the truth of the gospel of Jesus Christ. Paul told him, *"Be diligent to present yourself approved to God as a worker who does not need to be ashamed, accurately handling the word of truth"* (2 Timothy 2:15 NASB). Ministers should never

forget that the eternal destiny of countless people hinges on the truth of the gospel being faithfully communicated.

In reviewing some of the doctrinal categories listed above, Paul's comments to Timothy are weighted toward the simple facts of salvation through Jesus Christ. A summary of those statements includes:

- Jesus came to save sinners.
- God wants everyone to be saved.
- Jesus is the only mediator between God and humanity.
- Jesus gave his life to purchase freedom for everyone.
- Jesus was raised from the dead; this is the gospel.
- Jesus destroyed death and illumined the way to eternal life through the gospel.
- God is the Savior of all people, especially of those who believe.[1]
- Jesus Christ will someday judge the living and the dead when he comes to set up his Kingdom.

While the two letters to Timothy may not be as doctrinally detailed or as theologically robust as Paul's letters to Rome or Ephesus, or the epistle to the Hebrews, they are still substantive and highlight the essentials of salvation.

An effective minister, if he or she is to be a true representative of the Lord Jesus Christ, must be thoroughly grounded and deeply rooted in the great truths of God's word and the Christian faith. You cannot *"defend the faith that God has entrusted once for all time to his holy people"* (Jude 3 NLT) if you yourself are not persuaded of those truths. We may differ on minor points, but we should agree on the essentials of the faith, such as those that are expressed in The Apostles Creed:

> I believe in God, the Father Almighty, the Creator of heaven and earth, and in Jesus Christ, His only Son, our Lord: Who was conceived of the Holy Spirit, born of the Virgin Mary, suffered under Pontius Pilate, was crucified, died, and was buried. He descended into hell. The third day He arose again from the dead. He ascended into heaven and sits at the right hand of God the Father Almighty, whence He shall come to judge the living and the dead. I believe in the Holy Spirit, the holy catholic church,[2] the communion of saints, the forgiveness of sins, the resurrection of the body, and life everlasting.

While the above creed was not written by the apostles themselves, it has stood the test of time and remains as a good, concise summary of the rule of faith for the church in the early centuries.

The Greats Speak on Being Grounded in the Truth

Augustine

> "Where I found truth, there found I my God, who is the truth itself."

Martin Luther

"Peace if possible, but truth at any rate."

Blaise Pascal

"Truth is so obscure in these times, and falsehood so established, that, unless we love the truth, we cannot know it."

George Whitefield

"If we once get above our Bibles and cease making the written Word of God our sole rule both as to faith and practice, we shall soon lie open to all manner of delusion and be in great danger of making shipwreck of faith and a good conscience."

"Other men may preach the gospel better than I, but no man can preach a better gospel."

John Owen

> "The foundation of true holiness and true Christian worship is the doctrine of the gospel, what we are to believe. So when Christian doctrine is neglected, forsaken, or corrupted, true holiness and worship will also be neglected, forsaken, and corrupted."

Thomas Brooks

> "Truth is mighty and will prevail."
> "Where truth goes, I will go, and where truth is I will be, and nothing but death shall divide me and the truth."

Charles Spurgeon

> "Nothing makes a man so virtuous as belief of the truth. A lying doctrine will soon beget a lying practice. A man cannot have an erroneous belief without by-and-by having an erroneous life. I believe the one thing naturally begets the other."
> "Everywhere there is apathy. Nobody cares whether that which is preached is true or false. A sermon is a sermon whatever the subject; only, the shorter the better."[3]

Charles C. Ryrie

> "One of my former teachers repeatedly reminded us that an imbalance in theology was the same as doctrinal insanity."[4]

Francis A. Schaeffer

> "Truth demands confrontation; loving confrontation, but confrontation nonetheless."

Gordon Lindsay

> "The minister who has no deep convictions will flop around and drift with the tide. The central truth of the gospel is that Jesus died to save sinners and that signs will follow those who believe. That simple message must be delivered to mankind."[5]

Billy Graham

> "True Christianity finds all of its doctrines in the Bible; true Christianity does not deny any part of the Bible; true Christianity does not add anything to the Bible."
>
> "For centuries the Bible has been the most available book on the earth. It has no hidden purpose. It cannot be destroyed."[6]
>
> "Truth is timeless. Truth does not differ from one age to another, from one people to another, from one geographical location to another... the great all-prevailing Truth stands for time and eternity."[7]

Check-Up Questions

Are you firmly established in the basic, essential truths of Scripture? Are you clear on the nature of God, the Person of the Lord Jesus Christ, and his redemptive work? Are you solid on the inspiration of Scripture and the nature of salvation? Do you have strong convictions in these vital areas?

Notes

1. This phrase from 1 Timothy 4:10 has been wrongly interpreted by some to mean that all people will be eternally saved. God plainly *desires* all people to be saved (1 Timothy 2:4), and there is very much a sense in which God made *provision* for the forgiveness of all people. Upon seeing Jesus, John the Baptist declared, *"Behold! The Lamb of God who takes away the sin of the world!"* (John 1:29 NKJV). Similarly, the apostle John writes of Jesus, *"He himself is the sacrifice that atones*

for our sins—and not only our sins but the sins of all the world" (1 John 2:2 NLT). While God is the Savior of all people potentially, in that provision has been made for all, it is only realized and actualized when an individual receives that forgiveness by faith. God *"gave His only begotten Son, that whoever believes in Him should not perish but have everlasting life"* (John 3:16 NKJV). In this sense, he is the Savior *"particularly of all believers"* (1 Timothy 4:10 NLT).

2. The word *catholic* here does not refer to the Roman Catholic Church, but rather, to the Universal Church—the entire Body of Christ as a whole.

3. Charles Spurgeon, Preface to *The Sword and Trowel* (1888 complete volume), iii.

4. Charles C. Ryrie, *Balancing the Christian Life* (Chicago: Moody Publishers, 1994), Kindle edition, 9.

5. Gordon Lindsay, *The Charismatic Ministry* (Dallas: Christ for the Nations, 2013), 18.

6. Billy Graham, *Alone with the Savior* (Charlotte: Billy Graham Evangelistic Association, 2017), 15-16.

7. Billy Graham, *Peace with God* (Waco, TX: Word, 1953), 24. Copyright © 1953 by Billy Graham. Used by permission of Thomas Nelson. www.thomasnelson.com.

Chapter Seven

STAND AND DELIVER:

Preach the Word

"I did nothing; the word did everything."

—Martin Luther

KEY THOUGHT: Of all the various tools of ministry, perhaps none are more impactful than the teaching and preaching of God's word. It was the primary instrument of communicating truth by the prophets, by Jesus, and by the apostles, and it remains as a vital means of God conveying truth to the world today.

Paul wanted Timothy to be grounded in the truth personally (as discussed in the previous chapter), but he also expected him to communicate the truth faithfully to others—to teach and preach God's word. When Paul was initially leaving Ephesus, he envisioned serious doctrinal problems on the horizon. He had already sent Timothy up to Macedonia (Acts 19:22) and had left a group of elders in charge of the church. His prophetic warning to these spiritual leaders reveals the significance of the threat the Ephesian church would soon face.

> *I know that false teachers, like vicious wolves, will come in among you after I leave, not sparing the flock. Even some men from your own group will rise up and distort the truth in order to draw a following* (Acts 20:29-30 NLT).

What Paul foresaw certainly came to pass, and Timothy was later deputized by Paul to be his representative in overseeing the Ephesian church. By that time, many of those anticipated problems had taken root and were flourishing. Timothy had his work cut out for him!

False doctrines and false teachers were coming in from the outside and causing problems, and they faced internal problems as well. Some of the very people who Paul had earlier left in charge were teaching false doctrine and building their own personal followings. After Timothy had arrived and settled in Ephesus, Paul issued multiple admonitions to Timothy about his responsibilities relative to teaching and preaching; these are creatively compiled and synthesized below:

> *Timothy, I urged you to stay there in Ephesus and stop those whose teaching is contrary to the truth* (1 Timothy 1:3 NLT).

> *The Holy Spirit tells us clearly that in the last times some will turn away from the true faith; they will follow deceptive spirits and teachings that come from demons. These people are hypocrites and liars, and their consciences are dead* (1 Timothy 4:1-2 NLT).

> *The purpose of my instruction is that all believers would be filled with love that comes from a pure heart, a clear conscience, and genuine faith* (1 Timothy 1:5 NLT).

You have heard me teach things that have been confirmed by many reliable witnesses. Now teach these truths to other trustworthy people who will be able to pass them on to others (2 Timothy 2:2 NLT).

Work hard so you can present yourself to God and receive his approval. Be a good worker, one who does not need to be ashamed and who correctly explains the word of truth (2 Timothy 2:15 NLT).

Gently instruct those who oppose the truth. Perhaps God will change those people's hearts, and they will learn the truth (2 Timothy 2:25 NLT).

Preach the word of God. Be prepared, whether the time is favorable or not. Patiently correct, rebuke, and encourage your people with good teaching. For a time is coming when people will no longer listen to sound and wholesome teaching. They will follow their own desires and will look for teachers who will tell them whatever their itching ears want to hear (2 Timothy 4:2-3 NLT).

If you explain these things to the brothers and sisters, Timothy, you will be a worthy servant of Christ Jesus, one who is nourished by the message of faith and the good teaching you have followed (1 Timothy 4:6 NLT).

Teach these things and insist that everyone learn them. Until I get there, focus on reading the Scriptures to the church, encouraging the believers, and teaching them (1 Timothy 4:11, 13 NLT).

Teach these things, Timothy, and encourage everyone to obey them. Some people may contradict our teaching, but

these are the wholesome teachings of the Lord Jesus Christ. These teachings promote a godly life (1 Timothy 6:2-3 NLT).

If we establish the importance of a matter based on the frequency with which it is emphasized in Scripture, we can safely say that teaching and the proclamation of the truth is one of the most important activities in which a minister can engage.

Paul understood that certain leaders have a divinely imparted responsibility to teach the truth of God's word and to establish people in those truths, not to build the church around their own personalities. Paul's urgings for Timothy's teaching and preaching account for a large part of Paul's admonitions to Timothy. Paul makes his intention for Timothy clear at the very onset of the first letter: *"...I urged you to stay there in Ephesus and stop those whose teaching is contrary to the truth"* (1 Timothy 1:3 NLT).

The number-one way to stop darkness is to turn on the light. Likewise, the best way to stop error is to exalt and proclaim the truth. From all we read about Timothy, he was not an aggressive, confrontational type of person, yet he had a divine mandate to champion the truth.

Most ministers really prefer to be proactive in their teaching rather than reactive. Preachers (hopefully) don't want to be doctrinal policemen, just waiting to pounce on a truth infraction.

Ministers today likely recognize that there are no fewer errors and isms circulating in the earth today than when Paul first dynamically instructed Timothy to preach the word. The message of salvation through the cross was not praised by the populace in Paul's day; neither will it garner the applause of many today. Yet God's faithful servants have an unwavering mandate from God to proclaim Jesus in all of his fulness just as our spiritual predecessors have.

It is true that Timothy had to respond to and address certain problems that were rampant, but Paul wanted Timothy to know that he was not just fighting error for the sake of fighting error. Rather, promoting truth had a very positive purpose. We must never forget that truth—spoken in love—comforts, encourages, and lifts people. It instills hope and causes people to know the love and mercy of God. The word of God can and should be presented with authority, and yet with the greatest kindness and compassion toward the listeners.

To the Corinthians, Paul speaks of *"the foolishness of preaching"* (1 Corinthians 1:21 KJV) and said, *"We preach Christ crucified"* (1 Corinthians 1:23 NKJV). He proceeds to say that in his preaching, he *"determined not to know anything... except Jesus Christ and Him crucified"* and that he did not speak *"with persuasive words of human wisdom, but in demonstration of the Spirit and of power"* (1 Corinthians 2:2, 4 NKJV). Scripture makes it plain that God's ministers are not to preach for popularity or for the praise of others.

Keys to Connecting

As ministers, we should focus on making sure that what we are sharing is genuinely connecting with our listeners. This is more than simply asking, "Is my doctrine solid?" and "Are my points good?" Those have to do with us, but much of effective communication has to do with our hearers, and this brings us to two vital issues: (1) Do we know our audience and understand their needs? and (2) Are we really connecting with them?

I was recently doing a small graveside service that was comprised mostly of family members, and one of the ladies came up and explained that her eight-year-old niece was really struggling with the

death that had taken place; she asked if I could say some things in my remarks that would help this little girl. Moments like that remind me that the words we speak not only have to be true, but they also have to relate to those listening.

Though it was not in my notes, I remembered hearing the illustration of how astronauts put on a spacesuit when they travel into space. When they return from space, they no longer need that spacesuit, so they take it off and live here on earth. Likewise, while we are here on earth, we wear an "earth suit"—our body. When we no longer need that earth suit, we take it off and live in heaven. I added that to the committal service, and I believe it was helpful (perhaps to some adults as well).

Early in my traveling ministry, Lisa would sometimes remind me (relative to Sunday morning services) that I was no longer teaching full-time Bible school students or speaking at a conference of preachers, and she encouraged me to work on making my messages helpful to regular, everyday church folk, not just those who already had extensive knowledge of the Bible. I was reminded of Paul's statement, *"If you speak to people in words they don't understand, how will they know what you are saying? You might as well be talking into empty space"* (1 Corinthians 14:9b NLT).

Also, in 1 Corinthians 14:23-24 (NLT), Paul identifies three types of individuals who may be in attendance at church services:

- Believers
- The Uninformed
- Unbelievers

I began to review my notes and asked myself three questions:

- How much in this message would connect with and help a strong believer?

- How much in this message would connect with and help a young believer who knows very little about the Bible?

- How much in this message would connect with and help an unbeliever?

Of course, the Holy Spirit can take anything we say that is word-based and true and drive it home to any heart, but I was shocked to find that in terms of my own focus and preparation, I had given little to no thought to what would help an immature believer or an unbeliever.

I determined to make some adjustments and become more strategic in my teaching. Some people at this point might assume this is a reference to watering down or compromising the message, but that is not at all what I'm referring to. What I am saying is that the Bible describes scriptural content in terms of milk and bread, not just meat. We need to feed people spiritual food that is age appropriate.

From a church history perspective, Gregory the Great (AD 540–604) referred to himself only as "The servant of the servants of Christ." In his classic work, *The Book of Pastoral Rule*, he reminded the pastors he oversaw that in their preaching they needed to be very mindful of the types of people who would be listening to their messages on a given Sunday. Gregory writes, "According to the quality of the hearers ought the message of the teachers to be fashioned." He also said, "Every teacher should edify all in the one virtue of charity and touch the hearts of the hearers out of one doctrine, but not with one and the same exhortation."

In other words, he was telling them that while they never alter the truth, they should adapt their delivery to the audience. He told them to remember that the following types of people would be listening to their messages:

- Men and women
- The poor and the rich
- The joyful and the sad
- Servants and masters
- The wise of this world and the dull
- The forward and the fainthearted
- The impatient and the patient
- The kindly disposed and the envious
- The whole and the sick
- Those who fear scourges, and therefore live innocently, and those who have grown so hard in iniquity as not to be corrected even by scourges
- The too silent and those who spend time in much speaking
- The gluttonous and the abstinent
- Those that are at variance, and those that are at peace
- Lovers of strife and peacemakers
- Those who deplore sins of deed, and those who deplore sins of thought

In essence, the awareness and adaptability that Gregory advocated simply reflect the types of communication that Jesus did with those to whom he ministered. Simply think of the different ways Jesus ministered to different people, such as Nicodemus and the woman at the well.

This may make the job of a preacher more challenging, but it is a challenge to which we must arise. I hope it inspires us to not get in a rut in our communication, but to always strive to improve and be better. Of course, nothing takes the place of the anointing of the Holy Spirit, but we can also increase the effectiveness of how we use the tools God has given us.

How Long Should I Preach?

When I was a Bible school instructor, we had lab classes where students would give a twelve-minute sermon. Granted, that is not very long, but because of the number of students we had, that was the time allocated. Some students—especially those who had never preached before—were very relieved that they did not need to preach longer than that, but others expressed a desire to not feel so boxed in by the clock. That brings us to the issue of how long a sermon should be. I do not think there is an answer for that which fits every situation, so let's explore some of the considerations.

We always encouraged students, and even ministers, that people have a certain attention-span. With that in mind, it is best to preach long enough to make the needed points, but not so long that people feel exhausted and don't want to come back. Some of the attention-span issue is culturally (or experientially) based, and preachers should be attentive to how much their audience can receive in a service. It is counterproductive to wear people out and to exceed their ability to receive.

I remember when I traveled to a certain nation a few decades ago to speak at a conference for pastors. This country was experiencing revival at that time, and the spiritual hunger was very intense. This was

my first visit to this particular country, and I was shocked when the host informed me, "The pastors are really expecting great things this week, and they are very hungry. If you preach for less than three hours in any of your sessions, they will be very disappointed." As a Bible school instructor for many years, I was accustomed to fifty-minute class sessions, and the Bible school students handled three back-to-back fifty minute sessions very well, but these people amazed me in that they stayed completely attentive to messages that lasted three hours and sometimes, for an additional fifteen minutes beyond that.

Just because that was effective in one setting, though, does not mean it will work in other settings. I remember making the statement in one of my classes that if the Spirit of God is moving strongly in a service (and I was referring to an evening service at the time), that time restraints are not as important, but if nothing special is happening, the service should be dismissed at a reasonable time. A student came to me and referenced Paul preaching all night long at Troas (Acts 20:7-12). His implication was that if Paul could preach all night long, then we should be able to follow his example and preach long, extended sermons. I agreed with him that Paul did preach all night long, but at midnight, he had enough anointing to raise the dead (Eutychus). I told the student that if you have enough of the anointing of God's Spirit to raise the dead, that's one thing, but if not, you'd better close the service much earlier.

Obviously, Paul's visit to Troas was a very special occasion, and people knew that they might only get to hear the legendary apostle on this one occasion, so it was not a regular church service that they were able to experience week in and week out. We should be mindful that some things might work in some special types of services that would not work all of the time. Another exceptional situation occurred when Paul met with the Jewish leaders in Rome. When Paul arrived there the first time, he requested a meeting with these individuals to explain the Christian faith. Acts 28:23 describes what happened when this meeting took place: *"...Using the law of Moses and the books of the prophets, he spoke to them from morning until evening."* Again, this was a special meeting, not a regular, reoccurring event.

I know of a denominational supervisor who would coach and counsel the pastors in that particular organization. When they would complain to him that their churches were not growing, the first question he asked them was how long they preached during their Sunday morning services. They would often tell him they were preaching around an hour, and he told them bluntly, "You're not that good. If you'll preach shorter, more people will come." I'm sure many of those pastors felt their toes had been stepped on, but I heard that many of them worked on preaching more efficiently (and more briefly), and they often experienced church growth as a result.

Personally, I enjoy having forty-five minutes to preach a message, and I feel I can get a lot of good content in during that time window. Much of that is probably because I got used to having a fifty-minute time slot in nearly twenty years of teaching in a Bible school. However, as a guest minister, it is not uncommon to be allocated thirty or thirty-five minutes to deliver a message, and I've found that great content can be communicated in that time frame also.

Sometimes ministers need to do some introspection and evaluation about their time in the pulpit:

- Am I wasting time with unnecessary filler? I realize this is somewhat of a stylistic issue, but I have heard some messages that would be shortened by several minutes if the minister eliminated excessive usages of "Amen, Praise the Lord, Hallelujah, etc."

- Am I unnecessarily redundant? Some repetition can be good, but excessive repetition can lengthen the message without really adding anything to it.

- Have I really identified the purpose of that particular message? If my own thoughts are not clear about what is to be accomplished and conveyed, I will likely find myself wandering and stumbling through my own message. If I successfully identify the purpose of a particular message, then everything I put into that message should help establish and reinforce that goal. If it doesn't contribute to that purpose, I should probably leave it out.

- Am I going to see these people again? Several pastors have told me over the years that one of the ways they shortened their messages was to not try to tell the people everything about that topic in a single message. They will likely see many of the same people the next week, and they can use some of the content in subsequent messages.

How long was that message?

One helpful exercise is to consider some of the greatest sermons and speeches of all time. How long did they last? Here is a quick summary that we can look at as a reference point:

- 1½ minutes: Paul—Sermon on Mars Hill (Acts 17:22-31)

- 2 minutes: Winston Churchill—We Shall Fight on the Beaches Speech

- 2½ minutes: George Washington—Resignation Message

- 3 minutes: Abraham Lincoln—Gettysburg Address

- 3½ minutes: Peter—Day of Pentecost Sermon (Acts 2:14-39)

- 7 minutes: Franklin Delano Roosevelt—Pearl Harbor Speech

- 13½ minutes: Jesus—Sermon on the Mount (Matthew 5:3 – 7:27)

- 17 minutes: Martin Luther King—I Have a Dream Speech

- 17½ minutes: John F. Kennedy—The Decision to go to the Moon Speech

In the Bible, some of the sermons recorded are summaries of sorts. For example, after Luke records Peter's sermon on the Day of Pentecost, he then writes, *"And with many other words he testified and exhorted them, saying, 'Be saved from this perverse generation'"* (Acts 2:40 NKJV). We assume, therefore, that Peter's full sermon was actually longer than the 3½ minutes indicated above. However, the fact that Luke could give us an accurate and concise summary of Peter's message reinforces the idea that a message doesn't need to last forever to be effective.

In summary, I can't give a one-size-fits-all answer. Some ministers are able to hold the attention of people better (and longer) than others. Some congregations, because of their backgrounds, are used to longer or shorter messages. As a general rule, it is good to be respectful of the attention span of your people, work on improving your efficiency and effectiveness in speaking, and preach in a way that will make people hungry to come back and receive more in the next service. This is better than to exhaust them and have them wishing you had concluded your message much sooner than you did.

The Greats Speak on Teaching and Preaching

Gregory the Great (Paraphrase)

> The word of truth does not penetrate the mind of one in need if a compassionate hand does not deliver it to his heart. But the seed of the word flourishes and grows when the lovingkindness of the preacher waters it into the heart of the hearer.

Martin Luther

Luther gave the following advice to preachers:

1. Teach systematically.
2. Have a ready wit.
3. Be eloquent.
4. Have a good voice.
5. Have a good memory.
6. Know when to make an end.
7. Be sure of his doctrine.
8. Venture and engage body and blood, wealth and honor, in Word.
9. Allow himself to be mocked and jeered by everyone.[1]

"We ought to direct ourselves in preaching according to the condition of the hearers, but most preachers commonly fail herein; they preach which little edifies the poor simple people. To preach plainly and simply is a great art."[2]

"Some plague the people with too long sermons; for the faculty of listening is a tender thing, and soon becomes weary and satiated (stuffed)."

"Stand up cheerily; speak out manfully; leave off speedily."

"I would not have preachers torment their hearers and detain them with long and tedious preaching, for the delight of hearing vanishes therewith, and the preachers hurt themselves."

Philip Jacob Spener

"The pulpit is not the place for an ostentatious display of one's skill. It is rather the place to preach the Word of the Lord plainly but powerfully. Preaching should be the divine means to save the people, and so it is proper that everything be directed to this end. Ordinary people, who make up the largest part of a congregation, are always to be kept in view more than the few learned people..."[3]

· *John Wesley*

"Who is a Gospel Minister, in the full scriptural sense of the word? He, and he alone, of whatever denomination, that does declare the whole counsel of God; that does preach the whole gospel, even justification, sanctification, preparatory to glory. He that does not put asunder what God has joined, but publishes alike, 'Christ dying for us, and Christ living in us.' He that constantly applies this to the hearts of the hearers, being willing to spend and be spent for them; having himself the mind which was in Christ, and steadily walking as Christ also walked; he, and he alone, can with propriety be termed a Gospel Minister."[4]

"Explicitly preach the truth, though not in a controversial way. But... take care to do it in love and gentleness; not in bitterness, not returning railing for railing."[5]

"Give me one hundred preachers who fear nothing but sin, and desire nothing but God, and I care not a straw whether they be clergymen or laymen, such alone will shake the gates of hell, and set up the kingdom of heaven upon earth."

"Take care not to speak too loud, or too long. Never exceed an hour at a time."[6]

Jonathan Edwards

> *"First,* that he be *pure, clear, and full in his doctrine.* A minister is set to be a light to men's souls, by teaching, or doctrine. And if he be a shining light in this respect, the light of his doctrine must be bright and full. It must be pure without mixtures of darkness. And therefore he must be sound in the faith, not one that is of a reprobate mind. In doctrine he must show uncorruptness; otherwise his *light* will be darkness. He must not lead his people into errors, but teach them the truth only, guiding their feet into the way of peace, and leading them in the right ways of the Lord."[7]

George Whitefield

> "To preach more than half an hour, a man should be an angel himself or have angels for hearers."

Richard Baxter

> "We must feel toward our people as a father toward his children; yea, the most tender love of a mother must not surpass ours. We must even travail in birth, till Christ be formed in them. They should see that we care for no outward thing, neither liberty, nor honor, nor life, in comparison to their salvation."
>
> "I preached as never sure to preach again, and as a dying man to dying men."

Matthew Henry

> "An old sermon may be preached with new affections; what we say often we may say again, if we say it affectionately, and are ourselves under the power of it."[8]

Charles Spurgeon[9]

> "If we give our people refined truth, pure Scriptural doctrine, and all so worded as to have no needless obscurity about it, we shall be true shepherds of the sheep, and the profiting of our people will soon be apparent. If we speak as ambassadors for God, we need never complain of want of matter, for our message is full to overflowing. The entire gospel must be

presented from the pulpit; the whole faith once delivered to the saints must be proclaimed by us."

"Keep to doctrines which stir the conscience and the heart. Remain unwaveringly the champions of a soul-winning gospel. God's truth is adapted to man, and God's grace adapts man to it. There is a key which, under God, can wind up the musical box of man's nature; get it, and use it daily. Hence I urge you to keep to the old-fashioned gospel, and to that only, for assuredly it is the power of God unto salvation. Of all I would wish to say this is the sum; my brethren, preach CHRIST, always and evermore. He is the whole gospel. His person, offices, and work must be our one great, all-comprehending theme. The world needs still to be told of its Savior, and of the way to reach him."

"If with the zeal of Methodists we can preach the doctrine of Puritans a great future is before us. The fire of Wesley, and the fuel of Whitefield, will cause a burning which shall set the forests of error on fire, and warm the very soul of this cold earth. We are not called to proclaim philosophy and metaphysics, but the simple gospel. Man's fall, his need of a new birth, forgiveness through an atonement, and salvation as the result of faith, these are our battle-axe and weapons of war."

"Rest assured that the most fervid revivalism will wear itself out in mere smoke, if it be not maintained by the fuel of teaching."

"Blessed is that ministry of which CHRIST IS ALL."

"Brethren, first and above all things, keep to plain evangelical doctrines; whatever else you do or do not preach, be sure incessantly to bring forth the soul-saving truth of Christ and him crucified.

Your doctrinal teaching should be clear and unmistakable. To be so it must first of all be clear to yourself. Some men think in smoke and preach in a cloud. Your people do not want a luminous haze, but the solid terra firma of truth."

"Consider the condition of your hearers. Reflect upon their spiritual state as a whole and as individuals, and prescribe the medicine adapted to the current disease, or prepare the food suitable for the prevailing necessity."

"Bring in all the features of truth in due proportion, for every part of Scripture is profitable, and you are not only to preach the truth, but the whole truth. Do not insist perpetually upon one truth alone. A nose is an important feature in the human countenance, but to paint a man's nose alone is not a satisfactory method of taking his likeness: a doctrine may be very important, but an exaggerated estimate of it may be fatal to an harmonious and complete ministry. Do not make minor doctrines main points. Do not paint the details of the background of the gospel picture with the same heavy brush as the great objects in the foreground of it."

"It would be unwise to insist perpetually upon one doctrine to the neglect of others. We would give every portion of Scripture its fair share in our heart and head. Doctrine, precept, history, type, psalm, proverb, experience, warning, promise, invitation, threatening, or rebuke—we would include the whole of inspired truth within the circle of our teachings."

"Faithfulness demands that we should not become mere pipers to our hearers, playing such tunes as they may demand of us, but should remain as the Lord's mouth to declare all his counsels."

"I have no belief in that ministry which ignores laborious preparation."

"Your people need discourses which have been prayed over and laboriously prepared. People do not want raw food; it must be cooked and made ready for them."

"Preach upon practical themes, pressing, present, personal matters, and you will secure an earnest hearing."

"An old preacher used to say to a young man who preached an hour,—'My dear friend, I do not care what else you preach about, but I wish you would always preach about forty minutes.' We ought seldom to go much beyond that—forty minutes, or, say, three-quarters of an hour. If a fellow cannot say all he has to say in that time, when will he say it?"

"Brevity is a virtue within the reach of all of us; do not let us lose the opportunity of gaining the credit which it brings. If you ask me how you may shorten your sermons, I should say, study them better. Spend more time in the study that you may need less in the pulpit. We are generally longest when we have least to say. A man with a great deal of well-prepared matter will probably not exceed forty minutes; when he has less to say he will go on for fifty minutes, and when he has absolutely nothing he will need an hour to say it in."

"After he had been in the ministry over a quarter of a century, Spurgeon told his congregation, "I am still learning how to preach." The satisfied preacher will never grow. He will become the center of a mutual admiration society, not a source of spiritual power."[10]

"Spurgeon told about a man who preached for years in Hebrews. When he came to 13:22—'suffer the word of exhortation'—Spurgeon commented, 'They suffered!'"[11]

"The greatest force of the sermon lies in what has gone before the sermon. You must get ready for the whole service by private fellowship with God, and real holiness of character."[12]

"The kind of sermon which is likely to break the hearer's heart is that which has first broken the preacher's heart, and the sermon which is likely to reach the heart of the hearer is the one which has come straight from the heart of the preacher..."[13]

D. L. Moody

"It is very much better to get a reputation for being brief than to have people say that you preach long sermons. Say what you have got to say in just as few words as you can. Then stop when you get through. Some men go on and feel around for a good stopping place. I'd rather stop abruptly than do that. Don't waste any time. Remember, we are living in an intense age. Men think quicker than they used to... What we want in our preaching is to condense. Get a reputation for being short, and people will want to hear you."

Charles Finney

"Great sermons lead the people to praise the preacher. Good preaching leads the people to praise the Savior."[14] "My habit has always been to study the gospel, and the best application of it, all the time. I do not confine myself to hours and days of writing my sermons; but my mind is always pondering the truths of the gospel and the best way of using them. I go among the people, and learn their wants. Then, in the light of the Holy Spirit, I take a subject that I think will meet their present necessities. I think intensely on it, pray much over it, and get my mind full of it, and then go and pour it out to the people."[15] "I believe that all ministers, called by Christ to preach the gospel, ought to be, and may be, in such a sense so inspired as to 'preach the gospel with the Holy Ghost sent down from heaven.' All ministers may be, and ought to be, so filled with the Holy Spirit that all who hear them shall be impressed with the conviction that God is with them of a truth. Men and women vary indefinitely in their natural powers of persuasion; but no human eloquence can ever convert a soul. Unless the Spirit of God sets home and makes the truth of

God effectual, all human eloquence and learning will be in vain… Where this power exists, the more learning and eloquence the better. But it is painful to observe the constant tendency to substitute culture for this power, or human learning and eloquence in place of this Divine enduement. I fear this tendency is increasing in the Church. The Churches are calling for men of great learning and eloquence in place of this Divine enduement, instead of men deeply baptized with the Holy Ghost."[16]

Matthew Simpson

"[The preacher's] throne is the pulpit; he stands in Christ's stead; his message is the word of God; around him are immortal souls; the Savior, unseen, is beside him; the Holy Spirit broods over the congregation; angels gaze upon the scene, and heaven and hell await the issue. What associations, and what vast responsibility."[17]

G. Campbell Morgan

> "The supreme work of the Christian minister is the work of preaching. This is a day in which one of our greatest perils is that of doing a thousand little things to the neglect of the one thing, which is preaching."[18]

John Henry Jowett

In a series of lectures given at Yale University in 1912, John Henry Jowett spoke of an experience he had which reminds today's preacher not to be occupied with himself or herself.

> I went out early one morning to conduct a camp-meeting away in the woods. The camp-dwellers were two or three hundred men from the Water Street Mission in New York. At the beginning of the service prayer was offered for me, and the prayer, opened with this inspired supplication: "O Lord, we thank Thee for our brother. Now blot him out! And the prayer continued: Reveal Thy glory to us in such blazing splendor that he shall be forgotten." It was absolutely right and I trust the prayer was answered.[19]

Vance Havner

> "Make Jesus Christ your theme! I have seen preachers espouse causes and champion movements, and

> when the cause died and the movement collapsed, the preacher vanished too. But the man who glories in Christ never grows stale."

Warren Wiersbe

"A sermon need not cost us very much: a bit of reading, some main points (preferably alliterated), a few stories... and that's it. But a message is costly. 'Preaching that costs nothing accomplishes nothing,' said John Henry Jowett, and he is right. But David said it first, 'Neither will I offer... unto the Lord my God of that which doth cost me nothing' (2 Samuel 24:24). Unless the Word of God smashes through our own lives, burning and cutting, tearing down and building up, we have no right to give it to others. The man who can 'whip out' a sermon in a few hours on Saturday evening, after wasting a whole week of opportunity for meditation, may see what men call 'results,' but he will never see what God calls lasting fruit. A real message flows out of a broken heart, a heart open to God and to God's people. The man with a message steps into the pulpit saying: 'My heart is inditing a good matter: I speak of the things which I have made touching the king: my tongue is the pen of a ready writer' (Psalm 45:1)."[20]

"The writing of a sermon comes from learning; the preparing of a message comes from living. The ideal is a combination of both."[21]

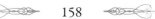

> "The next time you are tempted to question the centrality of preaching in your ministry, remember what the preaching of the Word accomplished in Martin Luther's Europe and John Wesley's England. Think of George Whitefield and Jonathan Edwards, Billy Sunday and Dwight L. Moody. And think of your hungry sheep who come week by week to be fed. Paul puts it so pointedly: 'Woe is unto me, if I preach not the gospel!' (1 Corinthians 9:16)."[22]

Billy Graham

> "When the Gospel of Jesus Christ is presented with authority—quoting from the very Word of God—He takes that message and drives it supernaturally into the human heart."
>
> "Preach with authority. The authority for us is the Word of God. Preach with simplicity... Preach with urgency... heaven and hell are at stake. Preach for a decision."[23]

Check-Up Questions

How much value do you place on the power and the significance of the word of God you teach and preach? Do you have an unwavering confidence in the power of the gospel and the inherent power of God's word to change and transform lives? Have you made it a point to excel in your delivery of God's word?

Notes

1. Martin Luther, *The Table Talk of Martin Luther* (Mineola, NY: Dover Publications, 2005), Kindle edition, 1692.

2. Ibid., 1727.

3. Philip Jacob Spener, *Pia Desideria* (Minneapolis: Fortress Press, 1964), Kindle edition, 1940.

4. John Wesley, "Thoughts Concerning Gospel Ministers," *Wesley's Works*, Volume X (Grand Rapids: Baker Book House, Reprinted 1978), 456.

5. John Wesley, "Minutes of Several Conversations Between the Rev. Mr. Wesley and Others, from the Year 1744, to the year 1799," *Wesley's Works*, Vol. VIII (Grand Rapids: Baker, 1979), 336.

6. John Wesley, "Letters to Mr. Adam Clarke," *Wesley's Works*, Volume XIII (Grand Rapids: Baker, 1979), 101.

7. Jonathan Edwards, "The True Excellency of a Gospel Minister," *The Works of Jonathan Edwards*, Volume 2 (Edinburgh, UK: The Banner of Truth Trust, 1974), 957.

8. William T. Summers, Compiler. *3000 Quotations from the Writings of Matthew Henry* (Grand Rapids: Fleming H. Revell, 1982), 222.

9. Unless otherwise indicated, all Spurgeon quotes are from his work, *Lectures to My Students*.

10. Howard F. Sugden and Warren W. Wiersbe, *Answers to Pastors' FAQs* (Colorado Springs: David C. Cook, 2005), Kindle edition, 838. Used by permission of David C. Cook. May not be further reproduced. All rights reserved.

11. Ibid.

12. Charles Spurgeon, *The Soul Winner* (Louisville: GLH Publishing, 2015), Kindle edition, 21.

13. Ibid., 54.

14. A. M. Hills, "Finney on Preachers and Preaching," *Biography of Charles Finney* (Cincinnati: Mount of Blessings, 1902).

15. Ibid.

16. Ibid.

17. Matthew Simpson, *Lectures on Preaching* (Phillips & Hunt, 1879), 98.

18. G. Campbell Morgan, *How to Preach* (New York: Fleming H. Revell Company, 1937), 7-8.

19. John Henry Jowett, "The Preacher in His Pulpit," *The Preacher—His Life and Work*.

20. Warren Wiersbe, *Listening to the Giants* (Grand Rapids: Baker, 1980), 353.

21. Ibid.

22. Howard F. Sugden and Warren W. Wiersbe, *Answers to Pastors' FAQs* (Colorado Springs: David C. Cook, 2005), Kindle edition, 837. Used by permission of David C Cook. May not be further reproduced. All rights reserved.

23. Russ Busby, *Billy Graham, God's Ambassador: A Celebration of His Life and Ministry* (San Diego: Tehabi Books, 1999), 55.

Chapter Eight

GOD'S HEART CRY:

Be Evangelistic

"I will not let you go: I have wrestled with God for my hearers in
private, and I must wrestle with you here in public."

—*George Whitefield*

> KEY THOUGHT: While the internal needs and
> responsibilities of the church are many, they must
> never undermine the once-given, always-relevant mandate
> to *"go into all the world and preach the gospel to every crea-*
> *ture"* (Mark 16:15 NKJV).

One of the simplest and most concise statements Jesus made about
his purpose in coming to earth is that he had come *"to seek and save those*
who are lost" (Luke 19:10 NLT). It is easy for ministers and churches
to become entirely absorbed in nurturing and caring for those already
found, but we must never forget the lost—those for whom Jesus died,
those who are yet to become his. Even though Timothy had great
internal responsibilities relative to the church, Paul reminded him to
"do the work of an evangelist" (2 Timothy 4:5 NKJV).

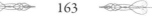

Philip is identified as an evangelist in Acts 21:8, and he is known for having shared the gospel with the lost—both publicly and privately. In Samaria, Philip *"preached Christ"* with signs following, and multitudes were ushered into the family of God (Acts 8:5 NKJV). After that, Philip was divinely directed to the desert where he *"preached Jesus"* to a lone traveler (Acts 8:35 NKJV). Just like the great numbers in Samaria, this individual also received Jesus as his Savior and was baptized.

Donald Gee refers to the office of the evangelist, saying "We all know and love men who seem to have the good tiding of God's redeeming grace burning in their souls. Whenever they preach, their favorite theme is salvation in its simplest form."[1] Timothy may not have stood in the *office* of the evangelist as did Philip, but he was nonetheless told to do the *work* of an evangelist. In a sense, every believer—the entire church—has been given what Paul calls *"the ministry of reconciliation"* (2 Corinthians 5:18 NKJV). Every Christian is called to be *"salt"* and *"light"* (Matthew 5:13-16), and this may be why Spurgeon said, "Every man here, every woman here, every child here, whose heart is right with God, may be a soul-winner."[2]

D. L. Moody, long known as a passionate soul-winner, related an experience that made a profound impression on him. On the night of the great Chicago fire in 1871, Moody concluded his sermon by posing a question to the congregation, "What will you do with Christ?" He asked them to consider that throughout the week and to come back the following Sunday. For some in the audience, the next Sunday never came. Even during Moody's sermon, the fire bells were ringing in the background, but because that happened periodically, no one thought anything about it.[3]

What happened that night was to be one of the worst tragedies in American history.

> The hall in which Moody spoke, the church he established, and his home were all destroyed in the inferno that became the Great Chicago Fire, along with more than 18,000 other buildings. But Moody hardly gave a second thought to his gutted home and church. They could easily be replaced—but not the lost souls. It was the memory of the audience he never saw again that was seared in his mind for the rest of his life. "What a mistake!" Moody later said. "Since then I never have dared give an audience a week to think of their salvation. If they were lost, they might rise up in judgment against me."[4]

Moody was forever changed by what happened at that time, and his son writes:

> From that time on [my father] laid great stress on the after-meeting, which took place at the close of an evangelistic address, in which he tried to bring individual souls to an immediate decision as to the great issues he had just brought before them. These meetings were probably the most characteristic and original feature of his work.[5]

What motivated Moody to be a soul-winner, to persuade people to decisively respond to the gospel, was compassion. W. R. Dale, a minister in England, said Moody "could never speak of a lost soul without tears in his eyes."[6]

A scriptural review of apostolic preaching reveals that when unbelievers were present, a strong appeal was made for them to respond to the gospel through repentance and putting their faith in Jesus Christ. For example, while Peter was preaching on the day of Pentecost, the listeners were greatly convicted, and they asked the apostles what they should do. Here is how this plays out:

> *Then Peter said to them, "Repent, and let every one of you be baptized in the name of Jesus Christ for the remission of sins; and you shall receive the gift of the Holy Spirit. For the promise is to you and to your children, and to all who are afar off, as many as the Lord our God will call." And with many other words he testified and exhorted them, saying, "Be saved from this perverse generation." Then those who gladly received his word were baptized; and that day about three thousand souls were added to them* (Acts 2:38-41 NKJV).

The people who had come under conviction had something to do. No, they were not saved by works, but in this case, repentance and baptism were actions springing from their faith. Verse 41 is key—*"those who gladly received his word were baptized."* Paul tells us, *"Faith comes from hearing, that is, hearing the Good News about Christ"* (Romans 10:17 NLT).

Peter's preaching on the day of Pentecost was designed to persuade. He testified and exhorted them to be saved (Acts 2:40). This is contrary to the idea that God just randomly, sovereignly, mystically saves those he wants to save and that we are basically uninvolved in the process. The story is told that when William Carey was contemplating going to the mission field, he asked a group of ministers if they sensed a responsibility relative to the Great Commission. One of the ministers replied, "Sit down, young man! When it pleases God to convert the heathen, he will do it without your aid or mine."

Fortunately, Carey did not sit down, but instead sailed for India and ultimately became known as the father of modern missions. From his arrival in 1793 until his death in 1834, the mission work he established was prolific in its accomplishments. According to Bennie Crockett,

> The Serampore Mission... created scores of Christian mission stations throughout southern Asia where missionaries distributed numerous Bible translations, established churches, and led people to a relationship with Christ... Carey's missionary understanding prompted him to translate the scriptures and Indian literature, and publish Bibles, grammars, and dictionaries in such Indian languages as Bengali, Sanskrit, Hindi, Oriya, Marathi, and Punjabi.[7]

One man's belief that the Great Commission should be fulfilled and that the lost should be reached produced so much.

We have a part to play because God *"took great delight in baffling the wisdom of the world by using the simplicity of preaching the story of the cross in order to save those who believe it"* (1 Corinthians 1:21 TPT). In addition to proclaiming the story of Jesus' death, burial, and resurrection, it is common to see words such as *pleading, persuading,* and *imploring* in the descriptions of Paul's preaching.[8] With every fiber of Paul's being, he desired that people become born again and fully devoted followers of Christ.

Leaders and servants are called to do many things in edifying the church, leading people in worship, creating fellowship opportunities, and teaching the word. However, reaching the lost must never be forgotten, ignored, or made a low priority. Let's love the lost, teach our people to love the lost, give lavishly to missions, and encourage creative and effective ways to reach people who come within our walls and those who do not.

The Greats Speak on Evangelism

John Wesley

"You have nothing to do but to save souls. Therefore spend and be spent in this work. And go always, not only to those that want you, but to those that want you most."

"What marvel the devil does not love field-preaching! Neither do I: I love a commodious room, a soft cushion, a handsome pulpit. But where is my zeal, if I do not trample all these underfoot in order to save one more soul?"[9]

"It is good to feed the hungry, to clothe the naked: But it is a far nobler good to 'save souls from death,' to 'pluck' poor 'brands out of the burning.' And it is that to which you are peculiarly called, and to which you have solemnly promised to 'bend all your studies and endeavors.'"[10]

George Whitefield

> "You blame me for weeping, but how can I help it when you will not weep for yourselves, though your immortal souls are on the verge of destruction."

Charles Spurgeon

> "I would sooner pluck one single brand from the burning than explain all mysteries."
>
> "If sinners be damned, at least let them leap to Hell over our bodies. If they will perish, let them perish with our arms about their knees. Let no one go there unwarned and unprayed for."
>
> "It is a very remarkable fact that no inspired preacher of whom we have any record ever uttered such terrible words concerning the destiny of the lost as our Lord Jesus Christ."
>
> "I believe that those sermons which are fullest of Christ are the most likely to be blessed to the conversion of the hearers. Let your sermons be full of Christ, from beginning to end crammed full of the gospel. As for myself, brethren, I cannot preach anything else but Christ and His cross, for I know nothing else, and long ago, like the apostle Paul, I determined not to know anything else save Jesus Christ and Him crucified."[11]
>
> "There ought to be enough of the gospel in every sermon to save a soul."[12]

> "Resurrection, then, is our aim! To raise the dead is our mission!"[13]
>
> "The business of the Church is salvation."[14]

Catherine Booth

> "Satan does not care what we do so long as we do not alert people to their sin. We may sing songs about the sweet by and by, preach sermons and prayers until doomsday, and he will never concern himself about us, if we don't wake anybody up. But if we awake the sleeping sinner he will gnash on us with his teeth. This is our work—to wake people up."

Hudson Taylor

> "The Great Commission is not an option to be considered; it is a command to be obeyed."
>
> "Would that God would make hell so real to us that we cannot rest; heaven so real that we must have men there, Christ so real that our supreme motive and aim shall be to make the Man of Sorrows the Man of Joy by the conversion to him of many."
>
> "Nothing can take the place of a real hunger for souls, or make up for the lack of it."

"I would never have thought of going out to China had I not believed that the Chinese were lost and needed Christ."

Alexander MacLaren

"If you would win the world, melt it, do not hammer it."

William Booth

"'Not called' did you say? 'Not heard the call,' I think you should say. Put your ear down to the Bible, and hear him bid you go and pull sinners out of the fire of sin. Put your ear down to the burdened, agonized heart of humanity, and listen to its pitiful wail for help. Go stand by the gates of hell, and hear the damned entreat you to go to their father's house and bid their brothers and sisters and servants and masters not to come there. Then look Christ in the face—whose mercy you have professed to obey—and tell him whether you will join heart and soul and body and circumstances in the march to publish his mercy to the world."

"Go straight for souls, and go for the worst."

"Most Christians would like to send their recruits to Bible college for five years. I would like to send them to hell for five minutes. That would do more than anything else to prepare them for a lifetime of compassionate ministry."

"Some men's passion is for gold. Some men's passion is for art. Some men's passion is for fame. My passion is for souls."

Andrew Murray

"So many are occupied with the hospital work of teaching the sick and the weakly in the Church, that the strength left free for aggressive work, and going forth to conquer the world, is terribly reduced. And so, with a finished salvation, and a loving Redeemer, and a Church set apart to carry life and blessing to men, the millions are still perishing."[15]

Oswald Chambers

"Oh, the skill, the patience, the gentleness, and the endurance that are needed for this passion for souls; a sense that people are perishing doesn't do it; only one thing will do it—a blazing, passionate devotion to the Lord Jesus Christ, an all-consuming passion. God grant that we may see that our passion for souls springs from that on which the Moravian Mission founded its enterprise: the fifty-third chapter of Isaiah; behind every heathen face, behind every face besotted with sin they saw the face of the Son of God; behind every broken piece of earthenware they saw Jesus Christ; behind every downtrodden mass of human corruption they saw Calvary. That was the passion that was their motive. God grant we may get it back again."[16]

A. B. Simpson

"One of the saddest and most common salves for guilty consciences on this line is the plea of the New Theology, and we fear the great mass of those who like to call themselves liberal Christians, that the heathen are really in no great danger after all, for God is too merciful to let them perish through the neglect of others in sending them the Gospel, and that there really is some other hope for them apart from the cross of Christ and God's plan of redemption. This is really an insult to the precious blood and the loving heart of Jesus Christ. If any less costly way of saving men would have sufficed, God would never have allowed His only begotten Son to be crucified. 'There is no other name under heaven given amongst men whereby we must be saved.'"[17]

C. T. Studd

"Some wish to live within the sound of a chapel bell, I want to run a rescue shop within a yard of Hell."

S. D. Gordon

> "If we lose the spirit of 'go,' we have lost the very Christian spirit itself. A disobedient church will become a dead church. It will die of heart failure."

John Mott

> "It is possible for the most obscure person in a church, with a heart right toward God, to exercise as much power for the evangelization of the world, as it is for those who stand in the most prominent positions."
>
> "No other generation but ours can evangelize the present generation."
>
> "Evangelism without social work is deficient; social work without evangelism is impotent."

W. A. Criswell

> "What is evangelism? It is intercession for the lost. It is the anguished cry of Jesus as he weeps over a doomed city.
>
> It is the cry of Paul, 'I could wish that myself were accursed from Christ for my brethren, my kinsman according to the flesh' (Romans 9:3).
>
> Evangelism is the heartrending plea of Moses, 'Oh, this people have sinned....Yet now, if though wilt forgive

their sin—and if not, blot me, I pray thee, out of thy book which thou hast written' (Exodus 32:31-32).

It is the cry of John Knox, 'Give me Scotland or I die.'

It is the declaration of John Wesley, 'The world is my parish.'

It is William Carey with his Bible in his hand and the burden of the world on his heart.

It is the prayer of Billy Sunday, 'Make me a giant for God.'

It is the sob of the parent in the night, weeping over a prodigal child.

Evangelism is the loving spirit of the shepherd who seeks the lost sheep, of the father who prays and waits for the prodigal son.

It is the secret of a great church.

It is the secret of a great preacher and of a great Christian.

A burden for the souls of lost men would bring to our churches a revival such as we have not known since the Spirit in fullness came on Christ's church at Pentecost.

To the end that our people might be saved, that our churches might live and grow, that Christ might be glorified and honored, let us give ourselves to the main task for which every minister is called and every church exists—evangelism, the hope of the world."[18]

Carl F. H. Henry

> "The gospel is only good news if it gets there in time."

Elisabeth Elliot

> "May we who know Christ hear the cry of the damned as they hurtle headlong into the Christless night without ever a chance.... May we shed tears of repentance for those we have failed to bring out of darkness."[19]

Billy Graham

> "Evangelism is not a calling reserved exclusively for the clergy. I believe one of the greatest priorities of the church today is to mobilize the laity to do the work of evangelism."[20]

Check-Up Questions

How is your outward focus? Is your church one that is mindful of the lost and emphasizes building relationships with those outside of the faith? If you preach, do you include targeted information for the lost in your messages, and are people given a clear opportunity to respond to the gospel? Are resources and energy going outside of the four walls of the church to reach the unsaved?

Notes

1. Donald Gee, *The Ministry Gifts of Christ* (Springfield, MO: Gospel Publishing House, 1930), 46.

2. Charles Spurgeon, *The Soul Winner* (Louisville: GLH Publishing, 2015), Kindle edition, 136.

3. Wilbur Chapman, *The Life of D. L. Moody: His Life and Work* (Harrington, DE: Delmarva Publications, 2013), Kindle edition, 1375.

4. D. L. Moody, *Moody's Stories: Incidents and Illustrations* (Chicago: Moody Publishers, 1899), 11.

5. William R. Moody, *Life of D. L. Moody* (Chicago: Revell, 1990), 488.

6. Ibid., 219.

7. Bennie Crockett, "The Life of William Carey," *The William Carey University Magazine,* (Spring, 2011), 4; https://www.wmcarey.edu/carey/carey-mag/Life-Legacy-spring-2011.pdf.

8. See 2 Corinthians 5:20 (NKJV); Acts 28:23 (NKJV).

9. John Wesley, "Journal," *The Works of John Wesley*, Third Edition, Volume II (Grand Rapids, Baker Book House, 1978), June 23, 1759, 491.

10. John Wesley, "An Address to the Clergy," *Wesley's Works*, Volume X (Grand Rapids: Baker Book House, Reprinted 1978), 496.

11. Charles Spurgeon, *The Soul Winner* (Louisville: GLH Publishing, 2015), Kindle edition, 57.

12. Ibid., 58.

13. Ibid., 82.

14. Ibid., 149.

15. Andrew Murray, *Working for God* (Heraklion Press), Kindle edition, 14.

16. Oswald Chambers, *So Send I You* (Grand Rapids: Discovery House, 1993), Kindle edition, 2985.

17. A. B. Simpson, *Missionary Messages*, Kindle edition, 40-41.

18. W. A. Criswell, *Criswell's Guidebook for Pastors* (Nashville: Broadman Press, 1980), 229. Reprinted and used by permission.

19. Elisabeth Elliot, *Through the Gates of Splendor* (New York: Harper & Row, 1958), 176.

20. Billy Graham, *Just As I Am* (San Francisco: HarperOne, 1997), 696.

Chapter Nine

THE POWERS
OF THE WORLD TO COME:
Supernatural Life and Ministry

"To us, as ministers, the Holy Spirit is absolutely essential.
Without Him our office is a mere name."

—*Charles Spurgeon*

KEY THOUGHT: Intellect and natural abilities are viable tools, but they will only take a minister so far. For ministry to be effective and lasting, a minister must have total reliance on the power and ability of God. We were never intended to carry out God's work in the finite limitations of our own wisdom and strength.

Supernaturally Called and Equipped

Christianity is a supernatural faith. Every true Christian has been born from above—by the influence and work of the Holy Spirit. Likewise,

the call to ministry is supernatural in origin, and ministers can only carry out their assigned work effectively by the enablement and empowerment of the Spirit of God. The presence of the supernatural, though, does not negate natural factors in our lives and ministries. For example, Timothy was no doubt influenced by the faith of his mother and grandmother (2 Timothy 1:5), but they could not save him or call him; only God could do that.

Paul reminds Timothy that it was God who *"saved us and called us with a holy calling..."* (2 Timothy 1:9 NKJV). It is important to remember that salvation was God's idea, not ours. It is true that we responded, but it is also true that God initiated the entire plan of salvation. God foreknew each of us, and Jesus had already died for our sins before we were even born. Likewise, he is the author and the initiator of our calling. That is why the Lord told the twelve, *"You didn't choose me. I chose you. I appointed you to go and produce lasting fruit..."* (John 15:16 NLT).

God's supernatural involvement in our lives continues into the way he equips and empowers us for service. Paul makes two specific references to the spiritual gifts Timothy received for use in ministry:

> *Do not neglect the spiritual gift you received through the prophecy spoken over you when the elders of the church laid their hands on you* (1 Timothy 4:14 NLT).

> *...I remind you to fan into flames the spiritual gift God gave you when I laid my hands on you* (2 Timothy 1:6 NLT).

In Timothy's situation, an impartation took place when hands were laid on him and a prophetic word was spoken over him. Though people were involved, this was something far beyond the will or

working of people. God supernaturally called and equipped Timothy, but he used others in the process. I have no doubt that God could work in a variety of ways in the spiritual journeys of different people, but this is how he worked in Timothy's life.

Perhaps no one ever prophesied over you regarding the call or the gifts that God has given you, but that does not mean God has not initiated such works in your life. It is good when people recognize and acknowledge God's working in your life, but what is most important is that you are faithful in using your gifts to serve others and to glorify God.

Supernatural Blessings

Not only was Timothy supernaturally called, but Paul spoke words of supernatural blessings over Timothy. In the second verse of the first chapter of both epistles to Timothy, Paul states, *"May God the Father and Christ Jesus our Lord give you grace, mercy, and peace."* It was very customary at the beginning of his epistles for Paul to speak a blessing using the words *grace* and *peace,* but to Timothy, Paul adds the word *mercy.* Perhaps I'm reading too much into this, but it makes me wonder if Paul didn't expand his normal greeting in writing Timothy because he knew that ministers need all the help they can get!

Supernatural Communication

As a child and servant of God, Timothy had both the privilege and the responsibility to pray. Paul admonished him:

> *Most of all, I'm writing to encourage you to pray with grat-*
> *itude to God. Pray for all men with all forms of prayers*
> *and requests as you intercede with intense passion. And*
> *pray for every political leader and representative, so that*
> *we would be able to live tranquil, undisturbed lives, as we*
> *worship the awe-inspiring God with pure hearts.... There-*
> *fore, I encourage the men to pray on every occasion with*
> *hands lifted to God in worship with clean hearts, free from*
> *frustration or strife* (1 Timothy 2:1-2, 8 TPT).

Prayer was addressed more thoroughly in chapter five, but it is always important to remember that personal communion and fellowship with God is spiritual oxygen to our souls.

Supernatural Empowerment

We already saw that Timothy received a spiritual gift (or gifts) when Paul and the elders of the church laid hands on him (1 Timothy 4:14; 2 Timothy 1:6). It was never God's intention that this impartation simply give Timothy a momentary feeling, but rather, that it would be a wellspring of divine ability throughout his entire life. The Amplified Bible indicates how perpetual this gift was to be in Timothy's life. Paul admonishes Timothy *"to stir up (rekindle the embers of, fan the flame of, and keep burning) the [gracious] gift of God, [the inner fire] that is in you..."* (2 Timothy 1:6 AMPC). The anointing of the Holy Spirit was to be a continuing source of power in Timothy's life.

In the very next verse, Paul elaborates on what God had placed on the inside of Timothy. *"For God has not given us a spirit of fear and timidity, but of power, love, and self-discipline"* (2 Timothy 1:7 NLT). Surely,

Timothy was meant to use all that God had put on the inside of him. Timothy was never meant to be launched into ministry in the Spirit, only to fulfill his assignment in his own strength and through mere self-reliance.

On the contrary, everything Timothy did for the Lord was supposed to be through the Holy Spirit's enablement. Paul instructed him, *"Timothy, my dear son, be strong through the grace that God gives you in Christ Jesus"* (2 Timothy 2:1 NLT). He did not tell Timothy to be strong in himself or to simply have willpower; he taught Timothy to rely on the grace of God that was in his life.

Clearly, Paul wanted the Holy Spirit to be integrally involved in every aspect of Timothy's life and ministry. He proceeds to admonish him: *"Through the power of the Holy Spirit who lives within us, carefully guard the precious truth that has been entrusted to you"* (2 Timothy 1:14 NLT). Ministry was not something Timothy was supposed to do in the limitations of his own natural resources and abilities. He was to carry out his work for God with the strength that God provided.

The Greats Speak on Supernatural Ministry

D. L. Moody

> "Our Gospel that we are preaching is a supernatural Gospel, and we have got to have supernatural power to preach it."[1]
>
> "If a man is not filled with the Spirit, he will never know how to use the Book. We are told that this is the

sword of the Spirit; and what is an army good for that does not know how to use its weapons?"[2]

"Your strength lies in God, and not in yourself. The moment you lean on yourself, down you go. The moment we get self-contented and think we are able to stand and overcome, we are on dangerous territory; we are standing upon the edge of a precipice."[3]

Oswald Sanders

"Spiritual leadership requires Spirit-filled people. Other qualities are important; to be Spirit-filled is indispensable."[4]

"Paul did not regard prayer as supplemental, but as fundamental—not something to be added to his work but the very matrix out of which his work was born. He was a man of action because he was a man of prayer. It was probably his prayer even more than his preaching that produced the kind of leaders we meet in his letters."[5]

"Prayer was the dominant feature of His life and a recurring part of His teaching. Prayer kept His moral vision sharp and clear. Prayer gave Him courage to endure the perfect but painful will of His Father. Prayer paved the way for transfiguration. To Jesus, prayer was not a hasty add-on, but a joyous necessity."[6]

C. T. Studd

"How little chance the Holy Ghost has nowadays. The churches and missionary societies have so bound Him in red tape that they practically ask Him to sit in a corner while they do the work themselves."

E. M. Bounds

"What the church needs today is not more or better machinery, not new organizations, or more novel methods; but men whom the Holy Spirit can use— men of prayer, men mighty in prayer."

Andrew Murray

"Christian worker, learn here the secret of all failure and all success. Work in our own strength, with little prayer and waiting on God for His spirit, is the cause of failure. The cultivation of the spirit of absolute impotence and unceasing dependence will open the heart for the workings of the abounding grace. We shall learn to ascribe all we do to God's grace. We shall learn to measure all we have to do by God's grace. And our life will increasingly be in the joy of God's making His grace to abound in us, and our abounding in every good work."

Philip Jacob Spener

> "It is certain that a young man who fervently loves God, although adorned with limited gifts, will be more useful to the church of God with his meager talent and academic achievement than a vain and worldly fool with double doctor's degrees who is very clever but has not been taught by God. The work of the former is blessed, and he is aided by the Holy Spirit. The latter has only a carnal knowledge, with which he can easily do more harm than good."[7]

A. W. Tozer

> "As a Christian minister, I have no right to preach to people I have not prayed for. That is my strong conviction."[8]
>
> "For a few seconds, picture in your mind the variety of wonderful and useful appliances we have in our homes. They have been engineered and built to perform tasks of all kinds. But without the inflow of electrical power they are just lumps of metal and plastic, unable to function and serve. They cannot do their work until power is applied from a dynamic outside source."[9]
>
> "Attention has recently been focused upon the fact that ministers suffer a disproportionately high number of nervous breakdowns compared with other

men. The reasons are many, and for the most part they reflect credit on the men of God. Still I wonder if it is all necessary. I wonder whether we who claim to be sons of the new creation are not allowing ourselves to be cheated out of our heritage. Surely it should not be necessary to do spiritual work in the strength of our natural talents. God has provided supernatural energies for supernatural tasks. The attempt to do the work of the Spirit without the Spirit's enabling may explain the propensity to nervous collapse on the part of Christian ministers."[10]

Vance Havner

"Too many times we miss so much because we live on the low level of the natural, the ordinary, the explainable. We leave no room for God to do the exceeding abundant thing above all that we can ask or think."

Charles Spurgeon[11]

"Praying is the best studying."

"Be yourself clothed with the Spirit of God, and then no question about attention or non-attention will arise. Come fresh from the closet and from communion with God, to speak to men for God with all your heart and soul, and you must have power over them.

You have golden chains in your mouth which will hold them fast. When God speaks men must listen; and though He may speak through a poor feeble man like themselves, the majesty of the truth will compel them to regard His voice. Supernatural power must be your reliance."

"If we had not believed in the Holy Ghost we should have laid down our ministry long ere this, for 'who is sufficient for these things?' Our hope of success, and our strength for continuing the service, lie in our belief that the Spirit of the Lord resteth upon us."

"Even so we have felt the Spirit of God operating upon our hearts, we have known and perceived the power which He wields over human spirits, and we know Him by frequent, conscious, personal contact. By the sensitiveness of our spirit we are as much made conscious of the presence of the Spirit of God as we are made cognizant of the existence of the souls of our fellow-men by their action upon our souls, or as we are certified of the existence of matter by its action upon our senses."

"We know that there is a Holy Ghost, for we feel Him operating upon our spirits. If it were not so, we should certainly have no right to be in the ministry of Christ's church. the ministry of Christ's church."

"To us, as ministers, the Holy Spirit is absolutely essential. Without Him our office is a mere name."

"We believe ourselves to be spokesmen for Jesus Christ, appointed to continue His witness upon earth; but upon Him and His testimony the Spirit of

God always rested, and if it does not rest upon us, we are evidently not sent forth into the world as He was. At Pentecost the commencement of the great work of converting the world was with flaming tongues and a rushing mighty wind, symbols of the presence of the spirit; if, therefore, we think to succeed without the Spirit, we are not after the Pentecostal order. If we have not the Spirit which Jesus promised, we cannot perform the commission which Jesus gave."

"The divine Spirit will sometimes work upon us so as to bear us completely out of ourselves. From the beginning of the sermon to the end we might at such times say, 'Whether in the body or out of the body I cannot tell: God knoweth.' Everything has been forgotten but the one all-engrossing subject in hand. If I were forbidden to enter heaven, but were permitted to select my state for all eternity, I should choose to be as I sometimes feel in preaching the gospel. Heaven is foreshadowed in such a state."

"We may not attribute holy and happy changes in our ministry to anything less than the action of the Holy Spirit upon our souls. I am sure the Spirit does so work."

"I am distinctly conscious of a power working upon me when I am speaking in the name of the Lord, infinitely transcending any personal power of fluency."

"May we full often feel the divine energy, and speak with power."

"But, oh, to burn in our secret heart while we blaze before the eyes of others! This is the work of the Spirit of God. Work it in us, O adorable Comforter! In our pulpits we need the spirit of dependence to be mixed with that of devotion, so that all along, from the first word to the last syllable, we may be looking up to the strong for strength."

"Our object is to drive the sword of the Spirit through men's hearts."

"Miracles of Miracles of grace must be the seals of our ministry; who can bestow them but the Spirit of God? Convert a soul without the Spirit of God! Why, you cannot even make a fly, much less create a new heart and a right spirit. Lead the children of God to a higher life without the Holy Ghost! You are inexpressibly more likely to conduct them into carnal security, if you attempt their elevation by any method of your own. Our ends can never be gained if we miss the co-operation of the Spirit of the Lord."

"The lack of distinctly recognizing the power of the Holy Ghost lies at the root of many useless ministries."

"A very important part of our lives consists in praying in the Holy Ghost, and that minister who does not think so had better escape from his ministry."

"The habit of prayer is good, but the spirit of prayer is better. Regular retirement is to be maintained, but continued communion with God is to be our aim. As a rule, we ministers ought never to be many minutes without actually lifting up our hearts in prayer. Some of us could honestly say that we are seldom a quarter of an hour without speaking to God, and that not as a duty but as an instinct, a habit of the new nature for which we claim no more credit than a babe does for crying after its mother. How could we do otherwise? Now, if we are to be much in the spirit of prayer, we need secret oil to be poured upon the sacred fire of our heart's devotion; we want to be again and again visited by the Spirit of grace and of supplications."

"I have opened my eyes at the close of a prayer and come back to the assembly with a sort of a shock at finding myself upon earth and among men. Such seasons are not at our command, neither can we raise ourselves into such conditions by any preparations or efforts. How blessed they are both to the minister and his people no tongue can tell! How full of power and blessing habitual prayerfulness must also be I cannot here pause to declare, but for it all we must look to the Holy Spirit, and blessed be God we shall not look in vain, for it is especially said of Him that He helped our infirmities in prayer."

"It is important that we be under the influence of the Holy Ghost, as He is the Spirit of Holiness; for a very considerable and essential part of Christian ministry lies in example."

"O to keep ourselves unspotted from the world! How can this be in such a scene of temptation, and with such besetting sins unless we are preserved by superior power? If you are to walk in all holiness and purity, as becometh ministers of the gospel, you must be daily baptized into the Spirit of God."

"Those who bind up the broken-hearted, and set free the captives, must have the Spirit of the Lord upon them."

"What position is nobler than that of a spiritual father who claims no authority and yet is universally esteemed, whose word is given only as tender advice, but is allowed to operate with the force of law?"

"Ministers, deacons, and elders may all be wise, but if the sacred Dove departs, and the spirit of strife enters, it is all over with us. Brethren, our system will not work without the Spirit of God, and I am glad it will not."

"It is certain that ministers may lose the aid of the Holy Ghost. Each man here may lose it. You shall not perish as believers, for everlasting life is in you; but you may perish as ministers, and be no more heard of as witnesses for the Lord."

"Brethren, what are those evils which will grieve the Spirit? I answer, anything that would have disqualified you as an ordinary Christian for communion with God also disqualifies you for feeling the extraordinary power of the Holy Spirit as a minister."

Check-Up Questions

How mindful are you of the supernatural nature of your life and work? Are you regularly aware of your reliance and dependence upon the Holy Spirit—that without his empowerment you could accomplish nothing? Can you cite recent examples of how he is working through, above, and beyond you?

Notes

1. D. L. Moody, "Power for Service." Sermon delivered at Tremont Temple, Boston, January 14, 1897.

2. D. L. Moody, *Secret Power*, Kindle edition, 29.

3. D. L. Moody, *To All People: Glad Tidings Comprising Sermons, Bible Readings, Temperance Addresses, and Prayer-Meeting Talks* (New York: Treat, 1877), 446-7.

4. Oswald Sanders, *Spiritual Leadership: A Commitment to Excellence for Every Believer* (Chicago: Moody Publishers, 2007), Kindle edition, 1484.

5. Oswald Sanders, *Dynamic Spiritual Leadership: Leading Like Paul* (Grand Rapids: Discovery House Publishers, 1999), Kindle edition, 1600.

6. Oswald Sanders, *Spiritual Leadership: A Commitment to Excellence for Every Believer* (Chicago: Moody Publishers, 2007), Kindle edition, 1615.

7. Philip Jacob Spener, *Pia Desideria* (Minneapolis: Fortress Press, 1964), Kindle edition, 1833.

8. A. W. Tozer, *Tragedy in the Church: The Missing Gifts* (Chicago: Moody Publishers, 1990), Kindle edition, 54.

9. Ibid., 4.

10. A. W. Tozer, *The Size of the Soul: Principles of Revival and Spiritual Growth* (Chicago: Moody Publishers, 1993), Kindle edition, 157.

11. All of these Spurgeon quotes are from his work, *Lectures to My Students*.

Chapter Ten

ULTIMATE ACCOUNTABILITY:

We Will Stand Before God

"Only one life, 'twill soon be past,
Only what's done for Christ will last."

—C. T. Studd

KEY THOUGHT: It is easy to get caught up in the moment of ministry and forget the eternal nature of what we are doing. We are often mindful of how others perceive us, but we must stay focused on the fact that we will ultimately answer to the Lord. At that point, the opinions held by others will be of little consequence.

Toward the end of Paul's final epistle, he acknowledges that his earthly trek is rapidly concluding and that he will soon be standing before the Lord.

> *And now the time is fast approaching for my release from this life and I am ready to be offered as a sacrifice. I have fought an excellent fight. I have finished my full course with*

all my might and I've kept my heart full of faith. There's a crown of righteousness waiting in heaven for me, and I know that my Lord will reward me on his day of righteous judgment. And this crown is not only waiting for me, but for all who love and long for his unveiling (2 Timothy 4:6-8 TPT).

Paul knew that a *"day of righteous judgment"* was awaiting him, and yet he did not fear or dread that day; he seems to have been greatly anticipating it.

In referring to the expected crown, Paul is borrowing terminology from the athletic games and is referring (as an illustration) to the garland wreath awarded to the winners in various events. Paul also says that this type of crown is not something exclusive to him as an apostle but will be rewarded to *"all who love and long for his unveiling."* This language seems to parallel Paul's reference to those who are *"looking for the blessed hope and glorious appearing of our great God and Savior Jesus Christ"* (Titus 2:13 NKJV).

Perhaps the aged apostle's optimism is because of what he knew—that he had fought his fight, had kept his course, and had kept the faith. I'm not implying that our entrance to heaven will be based upon our works—we are saved by grace through faith (Ephesians 2:8). However, I am saying that we will be—as the Bible says in several places—*rewarded* according to our works.

I wonder today how many believers and ministers live with the vivid awareness that they will one day stand before God and give an account for what they did in this life? How much would our decisions and actions be affected if we were mindful of the time when we will stand before the judgment seat of Christ. If we are to make decisions that are truly right, pleasing God must be more important to us than pleasing people, and principle must be more important to us than mere pragmatism.

I believe that much of Paul's steadfastness throughout his turbulent ministry was due to his focused desire to stand before the Lord and hear the words, *"Well done, my good and faithful servant."* May I encourage you to read carefully the following Scriptures and allow them to be firmly established in your heart? If you are ever tempted to get off course, I believe these can also speak to you and help keep you on the right track.

> ***For we must all stand before Christ to be judged.*** *We will each receive whatever we deserve for the good or evil we have done in this earthly body* (2 Corinthians 5:10 NLT).

> *So why do you condemn another believer? Why do you look down on another believer? Remember,* ***we will all stand before the judgment seat of God....*** *Yes,* ***each of us will give a personal account to God*** (Romans 14:10, 12 NLT).

> *Nothing in all creation is hidden from God. Everything is naked and exposed before his eyes, and* ***he is the one to whom we are accountable*** (Hebrews 4:13 NLT).

> *Obey your spiritual leaders, and do what they say. Their work is to watch over your souls, and* ***they are accountable to God.*** *Give them reason to do this with joy and not with sorrow. That would certainly not be for your benefit* (Hebrews 13:17 NLT).

What is your reaction when you read those divinely inspired statements about our accountability before God? It should create a healthy, reverential fear of God in our hearts and should cause us to walk very circumspectly before him.

It is important to remember that God is a righteous Judge. There will be no fooling him, even if we fooled others. He will judge righteously. This does not have to instill the wrong kind of fear, but it should be very sobering. The Lord will not be handing out participation trophies, but he will justly evaluate all that we did for him while on this earth. Having established that Jesus Christ is the foundation of all spiritual life, Paul addresses how we will be rewarded (or not) according to the quality of how we build on that foundation:

> *Anyone who builds on that foundation may use a variety of materials—gold, silver, jewels, wood, hay, or straw. But on the judgment day, fire will reveal what kind of work each builder has done. The fire will show if a person's work has any value. If the work survives, that builder will receive a reward. But if the work is burned up, the builder will suffer great loss. The builder will be saved, but like someone barely escaping through a wall of flames* (1 Corinthians 3:12-15 NLT).

The question in these verses is not our salvation. Even in the event of poor building, *"the builder will be saved."* Our goal, though, is not to simply make it into heaven (that happens by the grace and mercy of God), but to labor in such a way that we are deemed faithful.

Personally, I would prefer not to simply be *"saved... like someone barely escaping through a wall of flames."* Peter's description of the reward of the diligent is far more desirable: *"You will receive a rich welcome into the eternal kingdom of our Lord and Savior Jesus Christ"* (2 Peter 1:11 NIV). It is important, though, to realize that while salvation is a free gift, rewards are not automatic.

It is amazing that God has actually given us the criteria by which our works will be judged. We have a pretty good idea from Scripture what God will be looking for and at when our works are judged. In *The Work Book: What We Do Matters to God*, I have an entire chapter entitled "The Judgment of Our Works." I won't elaborate here, but I present seven factors that the New Testament indicates will be the criteria the Lord uses to judge our works.

They are:

> Our Motives (1 Samuel 16:7; Matthew 6:4, 6, 18; 1 Corinthians 4:5; Proverbs 21:2)
>
> The Royal Law of Love (James 2:8, 12; 1 Corinthians 13:1-3)
>
> Faithfulness (1 Timothy 1:12; 1 Corinthians 4:2; Matthew 25:21, 23, 28)
>
> Our Potential (Matthew 25:14-30; Romans 12:6)
>
> Knowledge (Luke 12:47-48; John 15:22, 24; James 4:17)
>
> Obedience (2 Corinthians 2:9; Hebrews 4:11)
>
> Quality (1 Corinthians 3:12-15)

There is a great temptation to get involved in judging others and critiquing their efforts for the Lord. However, we must remember Paul's admonition that we should not judge one another, but remember that we shall each give an account of our own selves before the Lord (Romans 14:10, 12).

Let me stress that the Judgment Seat of Christ is not something we should dread; rather, we can be joyful as we think about standing before him. I write:

> Believers should not dread standing before Jesus; rather, it's an event that we should anticipate with great joy. Imagine all those who have labored in love and served others with their lives being honored and rewarded by Jesus! This can not only give us hope for the future, but can motivate us today.[1]

This event has been solidly prophesied and foretold in Scripture. May we all live and serve in such a way that it truly is a source of joy and positive motivation for us.

The Greats Speak on the Judgment Seat of Christ

Thomas à Kempis

> "At the day of judgment, we shall not be asked what we have read, but what we have done."

Philip Jakob Spener

"Let us remember that in the last judgment we shall not be asked how learned we were and whether we displayed our learning before the world; to what extent we enjoyed the favor of men and knew how to keep it; with what honors we were exalted and how great a reputation in the world we left behind us; or how many treasures of earthly goods we amassed for our children and thereby drew a curse upon ourselves. Instead, we shall be asked how faithfully and with how childlike a heart we sought to further the kingdom of God; with how pure and godly a teaching and how worthy an example we tried to edify our hearers amid the scorn of the world, denial of self, taking up of the cross, and imitation of our Savior; with what zeal we opposed not only error but also wickedness of life; or with what constancy and cheerfulness we endured the persecution or adversity thrust upon us by the manifestly godless world or by false brethren, and amid such suffering praised our God."[2]

Jonathan Edwards[3]

"7. Resolved, never to do anything, which I should be afraid to do, if it were the last hour of my life.

17. Resolved, that I will live so as I shall wish I had done when I come to die.

> 19. Resolved, never to do anything, which I should be afraid to do, if I expected it would not be above an hour, before I should hear the last trump.
>
> 22. Resolved, to endeavor to obtain for myself as much happiness, in the other world, as I possibly can...
>
> 50. Resolved, I will act so as I think I shall judge would have been best, and most prudent, when I come into the future world.
>
> 55. Resolved, to endeavor to my utmost to act as I can think I should do, if I had already seen the happiness of heaven, and hell torments."

J. C. Ryle

> "Let us remember, there is One who daily records all we do for Him, and sees more beauty in His servants' work than His servants do themselves... And then shall His faithful witnesses discover, to their wonder and surprise, that there never was a word spoken on their Master's behalf, which does not receive a reward."

A. W. Tozer

> "Before the judgment seat of Christ my service will be judged not by how much I have done but by how much I could have done."

Billy Graham

"We will be judged according to the secret motives and the character of our work. If we have done our work for selfish motives or personal gain, even if the results looked noble to our friends and family, God knows our hearts."[4]

"Some of the most severe tests will be given to the [preachers] for the way in which they handled the Word of God. There will be no reward for leading others astray in lifestyle or in doctrine through false teaching."[5]

Check-Up Questions

How often do you think about standing before Jesus and giving an account of your work? If you were to stand before him now, how much of your work do you think would be considered gold, silver, and jewels, and how much might be considered wood, hay, or straw?

Notes

1. Tony Cooke, *The Work Book: What We Do Matters to God* (Shippensburg, PA: Harrison House Publishers, 2015), Kindle edition, 137. Copyright © 2015 by Tony Cooke. All rights reserved. Used by permission of Destiny Image Publishers., Shippensburg PA, 17257.

2. Philip Jacob Spener, *Pia Desideria* (Minneapolis: Fortress Press, 1964), Kindle edition, 609.

3. Edwards, the great pastor and theologian during America's first Great Awakening, actually wrote seventy resolutions that are recorded in his memoirs. Those listed here are a small sampling of that larger number. He began writing these as a young man and added to them periodically throughout his life. About these he wrote: "Being sensible that I am unable to do anything without God's help, I do humbly entreat him, by his grace, to enable me to keep these Resolutions, so far as they are agreeable to his will, for Christ's sake."

4. Billy Graham, *Facing Death and the Life After* (Waco, TX: Word, 1987), 264. Copyright © 1987 by Billy Graham. Used by permission of Thomas Nelson. www.thomasnelson.com.

5. Ibid.

Appendix A

TAKE HEED TO YOURSELF
by Richard Baxter

R ichard Baxter (1615–1691) was a highly influential English
Puritan cleric. The following is from two chapters dealing with
"The Oversight of Ourselves" in his classic work, *The Reformed
Pastor*. His admonitions reflect the wisdom and insights of a mature
minister who had seen many spiritual leaders fall and fail, and also the
concern and passion of a spiritual father who wanted to see ministers
thrive and flourish.

> **Take heed to yourselves**, lest you be void of that sav-
> ing grace of God which you offer to others, and be
> strangers to the effectual working of that gospel which
> you preach.
>
> **Take heed to yourselves**, lest you perish, while you
> call upon others to take heed of perishing; and lest you
> famish yourselves while you prepare food for them.
>
> **Take heed to yourselves**, lest your example contradict
> your doctrine, and lest you lay such stumbling-blocks

before the blind, as may be the occasion of their ruin; lest you unsay with your lives, what you say with your tongues; and be the greatest hindrances of the success of your own labors.

Take heed, therefore, to yourselves first, that you be that which you persuade your hearers to be, and believe that which you persuade them to believe, and heartily entertain that Savior whom you offer to them (Mark 12:31).

Take heed to yourselves, lest you live in those sins which you preach against in others, and lest you be guilty of that which daily you condemn (Romans 2:1).

Take heed to yourselves, lest you cry down sin, and yet do not overcome it; lest, while you seek to bring it down in others, you bow to it, and become its slaves yourselves...

Take heed to yourselves, that you not lack the qualifications necessary for your work. He must not be himself a babe in knowledge, that will teach men all those mysterious things which must be known for salvation.

Take heed to yourselves, lest you are weak through your own negligence, and lest you mar the work of God by your weakness (1 Thessalonians 5:19; Romans 12:11).

Take heed to yourselves, for you have a heaven to win or lose, and souls that must be happy or miserable forever; and therefore it concerns you to begin at home, and to take heed to yourselves as well as to others.

Take heed to yourselves, because the tempter will more ply you with his temptations than other men... He bears the greatest malice to those that are engaged to do him the greatest mischief As he hates Christ more than any of us, because he is the General of the field, the Captain of our salvation, and does more than all the world besides against his kingdom; so does he hate the leaders under him, more than the common soldiers... **Take heed**, Therefore, brethren, for the enemy has a special eye upon you.

Take heed to yourselves, lest he outwit you. The devil is a greater scholar than you, and a nimbler disputant: he can transform himself into an angel of light to deceive (2 Corinthians 11:14). You shall see neither hook nor line, much less the subtle angler himself, while he is offering you his bait. And his bait shall be so fitted to your temper and disposition, that he will be sure to find advantages within you, and make your own principles and inclinations betray you; and whenever he ruins you, he will make you the instruments of ruin to others.

Take heed to yourselves, because there are many eyes upon you, and there will be many to observe your falls. If other men may sin without observation, you cannot.

Take heed to yourselves, because such great works as ours require greater grace than other men's. Weaker gifts and graces may carry a man through in a more even course of life, that is not liable to so great trials. Smaller strength may serve for lighter works and burdens. But if you will venture on the great undertakings of the ministry; if you will lead on the troops of Christ against Satan and his followers; if you will engage yourselves against principalities and powers, and spiritual wickedness in high places; if you will undertake to rescue captive sinners out of the devil's paws; do not think that a heedless, careless course will accomplish so great a work as this (Ephesians 6:12).

Take heed to yourselves, for the honor of your Lord and Master, and of his holy truth and ways, lies more on you than on other men. As you may render him more service, so you may do him more disservice than others. The nearer men stand to God, the greater dishonor has he by their miscarriages; and the more will they be imputed by foolish men to God himself.

Take heed to yourselves, for the success of all your labors does very much depend upon this. God uses to fit men for great works, before he employs them as his instruments in accomplishing them. Now, if the work of the Lord be not soundly done upon your own hearts, how can you expect that he will bless your labors for effecting it in others?

Appendix B

MORE FROM JOHN WESLEY
on Ministry

Wesley responded to the question about "the best general method of preaching" with the following. He said that effective preaching should:

- Invite
- Convince
- Offer Christ
- Build up

Wesley continued by offering "smaller advices relative to preaching." I am including some of his recommendations and omitting others.

- Be sure never to disappoint a congregation, unless in the case of life and death.
- Begin and end precisely at the time appointed.

- Always suit your subject to your audience.

- Choose the plainest texts you can.

- Take care not to ramble; but keep to your text.

- Be sparing in allegorizing or spiritualizing.

- Do not usually pray above eight or ten minutes (at most) without intermission.

- Beware of clownishness, either in speech or dress.

Wesley proceeded to say:

> The most effectual way of preaching Christ is to preach him in all his offices; and to declare his law as well as his Gospel, both to believers and unbelievers. Let us strongly insist upon inward and outward holiness, in all its branches.[1]

Wesley's Twelve Rules of a Helper[2]

1. Be diligent. Never be unemployed a moment. Never be triflingly employed. Never while away time; neither spend any more time at any place than is strictly necessary.

2. Be serious. Let your motto be, "Holiness to the Lord." Avoid all lightness, jesting, and foolish talking.

3. Converse sparingly and cautiously with women; particularly, with young women.

4. Take no step toward marriage, without first consulting with your brethren.

5. Believe evil of no one; unless you see it done, take heed how you credit it. Put the best construction on everything. You know the Judge is always supposed to be on the prisoner's side.

6. Speak evil of no one; else your word especially would eat as doth a canker. Keep your thoughts within your own breast, till you come to the person concerned.

7. Tell everyone what you think wrong in him, and that plainly, as soon as may be; else it will fester in your heart. Make all haste to cast the fire out of your bosom.

8. Do not affect the gentleman. You have no more to do with this character than with that of a dancing-master. A Preacher of the gospel is the servant of all.

9. Be ashamed of nothing but sin: Not of fetching wood (if time permit) or drawing water; not of cleaning your own shoes, or your neighbor's.

10. Be punctual. Do everything exactly at the time. And in general, do not mend our Rules, but keep them; not for wrath, but for conscience' sake.

11. You have nothing to do but to save souls. Therefore spend and be spent in this work. And go always, not only to those that want you, but to those that want you most.

Observe: It is not your business to preach so many times, and to take care of this or that society; but to save as many souls as you can; to bring as many sinners as you possibly can to repentance, and with all your power to build them up in that holiness without which they cannot see the Lord. And remember! A Methodist Preacher is to mind every point, great and small, in the Methodist discipline! Therefore you will need all the sense you have, and to have all your wits about you!

12. Act in all things, not according to your own will, but as a son in the Gospel. As such, it is your part to employ your time in the manner which we direct; partly, in preaching and visiting from house to house; partly, in reading, meditation, and prayer. Above all, if you labor with us in our Lord's vineyard, it is needful that you should do that part of the work which we advise, at those times and places which we judge most for his glory.

Wesley indicated that the first, tenth, and twelfth in the above rules were the most important, but he was serious about all of them. Wesley's leadership style was certainly demanding and strict, and I wonder how such a leadership style would work in today's culture.

Wesley was extremely blunt and direct, as the seventh point indicates ("Tell everyone what you think wrong in him, and that plainly, as soon as may be; else it will fester in your heart"). Wesley certainly practiced what he preached, and modern readers would be pretty shocked at his overtness in confrontation, even toward his closest friends and associates.

John Wesley's Letter to a Minister

As early as 1755, Wesley had expressed great concern not only about John Trembath's ministry, but also his personal consecration to God. Apparently Trembath made some needed adjustments, but Wesley expressed other concerns in a letter written August 17, 1760. Wesley was concerned (among other things) about Trembath's lack of reading and how it was affecting his preaching:

> What has exceedingly hurt you in time past, nay, and I fear, to this day, is want of reading. I scarce ever knew a Preacher read so little. And perhaps, by neglecting it, you have lost the taste for it. Hence, your talent in preaching does not increase. It is just the same as it was seven years ago. It is lively, but not deep; there is little variety; there is no compass of thought. Reading only can supply this, with meditation and daily prayer. You wrong yourself greatly by omitting this. You can never be a deep Preacher without it, any more than a thorough Christian. O begin! Whether you like it or no, read and pray daily. It is for your life; there is no other way; else you will be a trifler all your days, and a pretty superficial Preacher.[3]

Wesley will never be remembered as a charming diplomat, but he spoke truth with powerful conviction and sought to help ministers become all they could be for the glory of God's kingdom.

Notes

1. John Wesley, "Minutes of Several Conversations Between the Rev. Mr. Wesley and Others, from the Year 1744, to the year 1799," *Wesley's Works,* Vol. VIII (Grand Rapids: Baker, 1979), 317-318.

2. Ibid., 309-10.

3. John Wesley, "Letter to Mr. John Trembath" in *Wesley's Works*, Volume XII (Grand Rapids: Baker, 1984), 254.

Appendix C

PREACHER SAVE YOURSELF

by Charles G. Finney

Charles Grandison Finney (1792–1875), one of the greatest evangelists in American history, composed the following. A few of the words in his original piece seem a bit antiquated and archaic to today's reader, and I have substituted what I believe captures his original intent in a few instances; these more modern synonyms appear in italics. His original work is the eighth chapter in his book, *Power from on High*.

> "Take heed to thyself, and to the doctrine; continue in them: for in doing this, thou shalt both save thyself and them that hear thee." 1 Timothy 4:16
>
> I am not going to preach to preachers, but to suggest certain conditions upon which the salvation promised in this text may be secured by them.
>
> 1st. See that you are constrained by love to preach the gospel, as Christ was to provide a gospel.

2nd. See that you have the special enduement of power from on high, by the baptism of the Holy Ghost.

3rd. See that you have a heart, and not merely a head call to undertake the preaching of the gospel. By this I mean, be heartily and most intensely inclined to seek the salvation of souls as the great work of life, and do not undertake what you have no heart to.

4th. Constantly maintain a close walk with God.

5th. Make the Bible your book of books. Study it much, upon your knees, waiting for divine light.

6th. Beware of leaning on commentaries. Consult them when convenient; but judge for yourself, in the light of the Holy Ghost.

7th. Keep yourself pure—in will, in thought, in feeling, in word and action.

8th. Contemplate much the guilt and danger of sinners, that your zeal for their salvation may be intensified.

9th. Also deeply ponder and dwell much upon the boundless love and compassion of Christ for them.

10th. So love them yourself as to be willing to die for them.

11th. Give your most intense thought to the study of ways and means by which you may save them. Make this the great and intense study of your life.

12th. Refuse to be diverted from this work. Guard against every temptation that would *lessen* your interest in it.

13th. Believe the assertion of Christ that He is with you in this work always and everywhere, to give you all the help you need.

14th. "He that winneth souls is wise;" and "If any man lack wisdom, let him ask of God, who giveth to all men liberally and upbraideth not, and he shall receive." "But let him ask in faith." Remember, therefore, that you are bound to have the wisdom that shall win souls to Christ.

15th. Being called of God to the work, make your calling your constant argument with God for all that you need for the accomplishment of the work.

16th. Be diligent and *hardworking*, "in season and out of season."

17th. *Dialogue* much with all classes of your hearers on the question of their salvation, that you may understand their opinions, errors, and wants. Ascertain their prejudices, ignorance, temper, habits, and whatever you need to know to adapt your instruction to their necessities.

18th. See that your own habits are in all respects correct; that you are temperate in all things—free from the stain or smell of tobacco, alcohol, drugs, or anything of which you have reason to be ashamed, and which may stumble others.

19th. Be not "light-minded," but "Set the Lord always before you."

20th. Bridle your tongue, and be not given to idle and unprofitable conversation.

21st. Always let your people see that you are in solemn earnest with them, both in the pulpit and out of it; and let not your daily *interaction* with them nullify your serious teaching on the Sabbath.

22nd. Resolve to "know nothing" among your people "save Jesus Christ and Him crucified;" and let them understand that, as an ambassador of Christ, your business with them relates wholly to the salvation of their souls.

23rd. Be sure to teach them as well by example as by precept. Practice yourself what you preach.

24th. Be especially guarded in your *interaction* with women, to raise no thought or suspicion of the least impurity in yourself.

25th. Guard your weak points. If naturally tending to *merriment* and *frivolity*, watch against occasions of failure in this direction.

26th. If naturally somber and unsocial, guard against moroseness and unsociability.

27th. Avoid all *pretense* and *phoniness* in all things. Be what you profess to be, and you will have no temptation to "make believe."

28th. Let simplicity, sincerity, and Christian *appropriateness* stamp your whole life.

29th. Spend much time every day and night in prayer and direct communion with God. This will make you a power for salvation. No amount of learning and study can compensate for the loss of this communion. If you fail to maintain communion with God, you are "weak as another man."

30th. Beware of the error that there are no means of regeneration, and, consequently, no connection of means and ends in the regeneration of souls.

31st. Understand that regeneration is a moral, and, therefore, a voluntary change.

32nd. Understand that the gospel is adapted to change the hearts of men, and in a wise presentation of it you may expect the efficient cooperation of the Holy Spirit.

33rd. In the selection and treatment of your texts, always secure the direct teaching of the Holy Spirit.

34th. Let all your sermons be heart and not merely head sermons.

35th. Preach from experience, and not from hearsay, or mere reading and study.

36th. Always present the subject which the Holy Spirit lays upon your heart for the occasion. Seize the points presented by the Holy Spirit to your own mind, and present them with the greatest possible directness to your congregation.

37th. Be full of prayer whenever you attempt to preach, and go from your closet to your pulpit with the inward groanings of the Spirit pressing for utterance at your lips.

38th. Get your mind fully *permeated* with your subject, so that it will press for utterance; then open your mouth, and let it forth like a torrent.

39th. See that "the fear of man that bringeth a snare" is not upon you. Let your people understand that you fear God too much to be afraid of them.

40th. Never let the question of your popularity with your people influence your preaching.

41st. Never let the question of salary deter you from "declaring the whole counsel of God, whether men will hear or forbear."

42nd. Do not *fail to speak definitively*, lest you lose the confidence of your people, and thus fail to save them. They cannot thoroughly respect you, as an ambassador of Christ, if they see that you dare not do your duty.

43rd. Be sure to "commend yourself to every man's conscience in the sight of God."

44th. Be *"not greedy for money."*

45th. Avoid every appearance of vanity.

46th. Compel your people to respect your sincerity and your spiritual wisdom.

47th. Let them not for one moment suppose that you can be influenced in your preaching by any considerations of salary, more or less, or none at all.

48th. Do not make the impression that you are fond of good dinners, and like to be invited out to dine; for this will be a snare to you, and a stumbling-block to them.

49th. Keep your body under, lest, after having preached to others, yourself should be a castaway.

50th. "Watch for souls as one who must give an account to God."

51st. Be a diligent student, and thoroughly instruct your people in all that is essential to their salvation.

52nd. Never flatter the rich.

53rd. Be especially attentive to the wants and instruction of the poor.

54th. Suffer not yourself to be bribed into a compromise with sin by donation parties.

55th. Suffer not yourself to be publicly treated as a *beggar*, or you will come to be despised by a large class of your hearers.

56th. Repel every attempt to close your mouth against whatever is extravagant, wrong, or injurious amongst your people.

57th. Maintain your pastoral integrity and independence, lest you sear your conscience, quench the Holy Spirit, forfeit the confidence of your people, and lose the favor of God.

58th. Be an example to the flock, and let your life illustrate your teaching. Remember that your actions and spirit will teach even more impressively than your sermons.

59th. If you preach that men should offer to God and their neighbor a love service, see that you do this yourself, and avoid all that tends to the belief that you are working for pay.

60th. Give to your people a love service, and encourage them to render to you, not a money equivalent for your labor, but a love reward that will refresh both you and them.

61st. Repel every proposal to get money for you or for Church purposes that will naturally disgust and *arouse* the contempt of worldly but thoughtful men.

62nd. Resist the introduction of tea-parties, amusing lectures, and dissipating *social gatherings*, especially at those seasons most favorable for united efforts to convert souls to Christ. Be sure the devil will try to head you off in this direction. When you are praying and planning for a revival of God's work, some of your worldly church-members will invite you to a party. Go not, or you are in for a circle of them, that will defeat your prayers.

63rd. Do not be deceived. Your spiritual power with your people will never be increased by accepting such invitations at such times. If it is a good time to have parties, because the people have leisure, it is also a good time for religious meetings, and your influence should be used to draw the people to the house of God.

64th. See that you personally know and daily live upon Christ.

WHY GOD USED D. L. MOODY

by R. A. Torrey

Though not as famous as Moody, Reuben Archer Torrey was an accomplished and highly effective minister in his own right. When the Bible Institute of the Chicago Evangelistic Society (now known as Moody Bible Institute) began, Moody called upon Torrey to become its first superintendent. He also served as the pastor of the Chicago Avenue Church (now known as Moody Memorial Church) from 1894–1906. Torrey engaged in many other pastoral, evangelistic, and educational works before his death in 1928, and is the author of more than forty books, including the brief work that follows.

Eighty-six years ago (February 5, 1837), there was born of poor parents in a humble farmhouse in Northfield, Massachusetts, a little baby who was to become the greatest man, as I believe, of his generation or of his century—Dwight L. Moody. After our great generals, great statesmen, great scientists and great men of letters have passed away and been forgotten, and their work and its helpful influence has come to an end, the work of D. L. Moody will go on and its saving influence continue and increase, bringing blessing not only to every state in the Union but to every nation on earth. Yes, it will continue throughout the ages of eternity.

My subject is "Why God Used D. L. Moody," and I can think of no subject upon which I would rather speak. For I shall not seek to glorify Mr. Moody, but the God who by His grace, His entirely unmerited favor, used him so mightily, and the Christ who saved him by His atoning death and resurrection life, and the Holy Spirit who lived in him and wrought through him and who alone made him the mighty power that he was to this world. Furthermore: I hope to make it clear that the God who used D. L. Moody in his day is just as ready to use you and me, in this day, if we, on our part, do what D. L. Moody did, which was what made it possible for God to so abundantly use him.

The whole secret of why D. L. Moody was such a mightily used man you will find in Psalm 62:11: "God hath spoken once; twice have I heard this; that POWER BELONGETH UNTO GOD." I am glad it does. I am glad that power did not belong to D. L. Moody; I am glad that it did not belong to Charles G. Finney; I am glad that it did not belong to Martin Luther; I am glad that it did not belong to any other Christian man whom God has greatly used in this world's history. Power belongs to God. If D. L. Moody had any power, and he had great power, he got it from God.

But God does not give His power arbitrarily. It is true that He gives it to whomsoever He will, but He wills to give it on certain conditions, which are clearly revealed in His Word; and D. L. Moody met those conditions and God made him the most wonderful preacher of his generation; yes, I think the most wonderful man of his generation.

But how was it that D. L. Moody had that power of God so wonderfully manifested in his life? Pondering this question it seemed

to me that there were seven things in the life of D. L. Moody that accounted for God's using him so largely as He did.

1. A Fully Surrendered Man

The first thing that accounts for God's using D. L. Moody so mightily was that he was a fully surrendered man. Every ounce of that two-hundred-and-eighty-pound body of his belonged to God; everything he was and everything he had, belonged wholly to God. Now, I am not saying that Mr. Moody was perfect; he was not. If I attempted to, I presume I could point out some defects in his character. It does not occur to me at this moment what they were; but I am confident that I could think of some, if I tried real hard. I have never yet met a perfect man, not one. I have known perfect men in the sense in which the Bible commands us to be perfect, i.e., men who are wholly God's, out and out for God, fully surrendered to God, with no will but God's will; but I have never known a man in whom I could not see some defects, some places where he might have been improved.

No, Mr. Moody was not a faultless man. If he had any flaws in his character, and he had, I presume I was in a position to know them better than almost any other man, because of my very close association with him in the later years of his life; and furthermore, I suppose that in his latter days he opened his heart to me more fully than to anyone else in the world. I think He told me some things that he told no one else. I presume I knew whatever defects there were in his character as well as anybody. But while I recognized such flaws, nevertheless, I know that he was a man who belonged wholly to God.

The first month I was in Chicago, we were having a talk about something upon which we very widely differed, and Mr. Moody turned to me very frankly and very kindly and said in defense of his own position: "Torrey, if I believed that God wanted me to jump out of that window, I would jump." I believe he would. If he thought God wanted him to do anything, he would do it. He belonged wholly, unreservedly, unqualifiedly, entirely, to God.

Henry Varley, a very intimate friend of Mr. Moody in the earlier days of his work, loved to tell how he once said to him: "It remains to be seen what God will do with a man who gives himself up wholly to Him." I am told that when Mr. Henry Varley said that, Mr. Moody said to himself: "Well, I will be that man." And I, for my part, do not think "it remains to be seen" what God will do with a man who gives himself up wholly to Him. I think it has been seen already in D. L. Moody.

If you and I are to be used in our sphere as D. L. Moody was used in his, we must put all that we have and all that we are in the hands of God, for Him to use as He will, to send us where He will, for God to do with us what He will, and we, on our part, to do everything God bids us do.

There are thousands and tens of thousands of men and women in Christian work, brilliant men and women, rarely gifted men and women, men and women who are making great sacrifices, men and women who have put all conscious sin out of their lives, yet who, nevertheless, have stopped short of absolute surrender to God, and therefore have stopped short of fullness of power. But Mr. Moody did not stop short of absolute surrender to God; he was a wholly surrendered man, and if you and I are to be used, you and I must be wholly surrendered men and women.

2. A Man of Prayer

The second secret of the great power exhibited in Mr. Moody's life was that Mr. Moody was in the deepest and most meaningful sense a man of prayer. People oftentimes say to me: "Well, I went many miles to see and to hear D. L. Moody and he certainly was a wonderful preacher." Yes, D. L. Moody certainly was a wonderful preacher; taking it all in all, the most wonderful preacher I have ever heard, and it was a great privilege to hear him preach as he alone could preach; but out of a very intimate acquaintance with him I wish to testify that he was a far greater pray-er than he was preacher.

Time and time again, he was confronted by obstacles that seemed insurmountable, but he always knew the way to surmount and to overcome all difficulties. He knew the way to bring to pass anything that needed to be brought to pass. He knew and believed in the deepest depths of his soul that "nothing was too hard for the Lord" and that prayer could do anything that God could do.

Oftentimes Mr. Moody would write me when he was about to undertake some new work, saying: "I am beginning work in such and such a place on such and such a day; I wish you would get the students together for a day of fasting and prayer." And often I have taken those letters and read them to the students in the lecture room and said: "Mr. Moody wants us to have a day of fasting and prayer, first for God's blessing on our own souls and work, and then for God's blessing on him and his work."

Often we were gathered in the lecture room far into the night—sometimes till one, two, three, four or even five o'clock in the morning, crying to God, just because Mr. Moody urged us to wait upon God until we received His blessing. How many men and women I have known whose lives and characters have been transformed by those nights of prayer and who have wrought mighty things in many lands because of those nights of prayer!

One day Mr. Moody drove up to my house at Northfield and said: "Torrey, I want you to take a ride with me." I got into the carriage and we drove out toward Lover's Lane, talking about some great and unexpected difficulties that had arisen in regard to the work in Northfield and Chicago, and in connection with other work that was very dear to him.

As we drove along, some black storm clouds lay ahead of us, and then suddenly, as we were talking, it began to rain. He drove the horse into a shed near the entrance to Lover's Lane to shelter the horse, and then laid the reins upon the dashboard and said: "Torrey, pray"; and then, as best I could, I prayed, while he in his heart joined me in prayer. And when my voice was silent he began to pray. Oh, I wish you could have heard that prayer! I shall never forget it, so simple, so trustful, so definite and so direct and so mighty. When the storm was over and we drove back to town, the obstacles had been surmounted, and the work of the schools, and other work that was threatened, went on as it had never gone on before, and it has gone on until this day.

As we drove back, Mr. Moody said to me: "Torrey, we will let the other men do the talking and the criticizing, and we will stick to the work that God has given us to do, and let Him take care of the difficulties and answer the criticisms."

On one occasion Mr. Moody said to me in Chicago: "I have just found, to my surprise, that we are twenty thousand dollars behind in our finances for the work here and in Northfield, and we must have that twenty thousand dollars, and I am going to get it by prayer." He did not tell a soul who had the ability to give a penny of the twenty thousand dollars' deficit, but looked right to God and said: "I need twenty thousand dollars for my work; send me that money in such a way that I will know it comes straight from Thee." And God heard that prayer. The money came in such a way that it was clear that it came from God in direct answer to prayer.

Yes, D. L. Moody was a man who believed in the God who answers prayer, and not only believed in Him in a theoretical way but believed in Him in a practical way. He was a man who met every difficulty that stood in his way—by prayer. Everything he undertook was backed up by prayer, and in everything, his ultimate dependence was upon God.

3. A Deep and Practical Student of the Bible

The third secret of Mr. Moody's power, or the third reason why God used D. L. Moody, was because he was a deep and practical student of the Word of God. Nowadays it is often said of D. L. Moody that he was not a student. I wish to say that he was a student; most emphatically he was a student. He was not a student of psychology; he was not a student of anthropology—I am very sure he would not have known what that word meant; he was not a student of biology; he was not a student of philosophy; he was not even a student of theology, in the technical sense of the term; but he was a student, a profound and practical student of the one Book that is more worth studying than all other books in the world put together; he was a student of the Bible.

Every day of his life, I have reason for believing, he arose very early in the morning to study the Word of God, way down to the close of his life. Mr. Moody used to rise about four o'clock in the morning to study the Bible. He would say to me: "If I am going to get in any study, I have got to get up before the other folks get up"; and he would shut himself up in a remote room in his house, alone with his God and his Bible.

229

I shall never forget the first night I spent in his home. He had invited me to take the superintendency of the Bible Institute and I had already begun my work; I was on my way to some city in the East to preside at the International Christian Workers' Convention. He wrote me saying: "Just as soon as the Convention is over, come up to Northfield." He learned when I was likely to arrive and drove over to South Vernon to meet me. That night he had all the teachers from the Mount Hermon School and from the Northfield Seminary come together at the house to meet me, and to talk over the problems of the two schools. We talked together far on into the night, and then, after the principals and teachers of the schools had gone home, Mr. Moody and I talked together about the problems a while longer.

It was very late when I got to bed that night, but very early the next morning, about five o'clock, I heard a gentle tap on my door. Then I heard Mr. Moody's voice whispering: "Torrey, are you up?" I happened to be; I do not always get up at that early hour but I happened to be up that particular morning. He said: "I want you to go somewhere with me," and I went down with him. Then I found out that he had already been up an hour or two in his room studying the Word of God.

Oh, you may talk about power; but, if you neglect the one Book that God has given you as the one instrument through which He imparts and exercises His power, you will not have it. You may read many books and go to many conventions and you may have your all-night prayer meetings to pray for the power of the Holy Ghost; but unless you keep in constant and close association with the one Book, the Bible, you will not have power. And if you ever had power, you will not maintain it except by the daily, earnest, intense study of that Book.

Ninety-nine Christians in every hundred are merely playing at Bible study; and therefore ninety-nine Christians in every hundred are mere weaklings, when they might be giants, both in their Christian life and in their service.

It was largely because of his thorough knowledge of the Bible, and his practical knowledge of the Bible, that Mr. Moody drew such immense crowds. On "Chicago Day," in October, 1893, none of the theaters of Chicago dared to open because it was expected that everybody in Chicago would go on that day to the World's Fair; and, in point of fact, something like four hundred thousand people did pass through the gates of the Fair that day. Everybody in Chicago was expected to be at that end of the city on that day. But Mr. Moody said to me: "Torrey, engage the Central Music Hall and announce meetings from nine o'clock in the morning till six o'clock at night." "Why," I replied, "Mr. Moody, nobody will be at this end of Chicago on that day; not even the theaters dare to open; everybody is going down to Jackson Park to the Fair; we cannot get anybody out on this day."

Mr. Moody replied: "You do as you are told"; and I did as I was told and engaged the Central Music Hall for continuous meetings from nine o'clock in the morning till six o'clock at night. But I did it with a heavy heart; I thought there would be poor audiences. I was on the program at noon that day. Being very busy in my office about the details of the campaign, I did not reach the Central Music Hall till almost noon. I thought I would have no trouble in getting in. But when I got almost to the Hall I found to my amazement that not only was it packed but the vestibule was packed and the steps were packed, and there was no getting anywhere near the door; and if I had not gone round and climbed in a back window they would have lost their speaker for that hour. But that would not have been of much importance, for the crowds had not gathered to hear me; it was the magic of Mr. Moody's name that had drawn them. And why did they long to hear Mr. Moody? Because they knew that while he was not versed in many of the philosophies and fads and fancies of the day, he did know the one Book that this old world most longs to know—the Bible.

I shall never forget Moody's last visit to Chicago. The ministers of Chicago had sent me to Cincinnati to invite him to come to Chicago and hold a meeting. In response to the invitation, Mr. Moody said to me: "If you will hire the Auditorium for weekday mornings and afternoons and have meetings at ten in the morning and three in the afternoon, I will go." I replied: "Mr. Moody, you know what a busy city Chicago is, and how impossible it is for businessmen to get out at ten o'clock in the morning and three in the afternoon on working days. Will you not hold evening meetings and meetings on Sunday?" "No," he replied, "I am afraid if I did, I would interfere with the regular work of the churches."

I went back to Chicago and engaged the Auditorium, which at that time was the building having the largest seating capacity of any building in the city, seating in those days about seven thousand people; I announced weekday meetings, with Mr. Moody as the speaker, at ten o'clock in the mornings and three o'clock in the afternoons.

At once protests began to pour in upon me. One of them came from Marshall Field, at that time the business king of Chicago. "Mr. Torrey," Mr. Field wrote, "we businessmen of Chicago wish to hear Mr. Moody, and you know perfectly well how impossible it is for us to get out at ten o'clock in the morning and three o'clock in the afternoon; have evening meetings." I received many letters of a similar purport and wrote to Mr. Moody urging him to give us evening meetings. But Mr. Moody simply replied: "You do as you are told," and I did as I was told; that is the way I kept my job.

On the first morning of the meetings I went down to the Auditorium about half an hour before the appointed time, but I went with much fear and apprehension; I thought the Auditorium would be nowhere nearly full. When I reached there, to my amazement I found a queue of people four abreast extending from the Congress Street entrance to Wabash Avenue, then a block north on Wabash Avenue, then a break to let traffic through, and then another block, and so on. I went in through the back door, and there were many clamoring for entrance there. When the doors were opened at the appointed time, we had a cordon of twenty policemen to keep back the crowd; but the crowd was so great that it swept the cordon of policemen off their feet and packed eight thousand people into the building before we could get the doors shut. And I think there were as many left on the outside as there were in the building. I do not think that anyone else in the world could have drawn such a crowd at such a time.

Why? Because though Mr. Moody knew little about science or philosophy or literature in general, he did know the one Book that this old world is perishing to know and longing to know; and this old world will flock to hear men who know the Bible and preach the Bible as they will flock to hear nothing else on earth.

During all the months of the World's Fair in Chicago, no one could draw such crowds as Mr. Moody. Judging by the papers, one would have thought that the great religious event in Chicago at that time was the World's Congress of Religions. One very gifted man of letters in the East was invited to speak at this Congress. He saw in this invitation the opportunity of his life and prepared his paper, the exact title of which I do not now recall, but it was something along the line of "New Light on the Old Doctrines." He prepared the paper with great care, and then sent it around to his most trusted and gifted friends for criticisms. These men sent it back to him with such emendations as they had to suggest. Then he rewrote the paper, incorporating as many of the suggestions and criticisms as seemed wise. Then he sent it around for further criticisms. Then he wrote the paper a third time, and had it, as he trusted, perfect. He went on to Chicago to meet this coveted opportunity of speaking at the World's Congress of Religions.

It was at eleven o'clock on a Saturday morning (if I remember correctly) that he was to speak. He stood outside the door of the platform waiting for the great moment to arrive, and as the clock struck eleven he walked on to the platform to face a magnificent audience of eleven women and two men! But there was not a building anywhere in Chicago that would accommodate the very same day the crowds that would flock to hear Mr. Moody at any hour of the day or night.

Oh, men and women, if you wish to get an audience and wish to do that audience some good after you get them, study, study, STUDY the one Book, and preach, preach, PREACH the one Book, and teach, teach, TEACH the one Book, the Bible, the only Book that is God's Word, and the only Book that has power to gather and hold and bless the crowds for any great length of time.

4. A Humble Man

The fourth reason why God continuously, through so many years, used D. L. Moody was because he was a humble man. I think D. L. Moody was the humblest man I ever knew in all my life. He loved to quote the words of another; "Faith gets the most; love works the most; but humility keeps the most."

He himself had the humility that keeps everything it gets. As I have already said, he was the most humble man I ever knew, i.e., the most humble man when we bear in mind the great things that he did, and the praise that was lavished upon him. Oh, how he loved to put himself in the background and put other men in the foreground.

How often he would stand on a platform with some of us little fellows seated behind him and as he spoke he would say: "There are better men coming after me." As he said it, he would point back over his shoulder with his thumb to the "little fellows." I do not know how he could believe it, but he really did believe that the others that were coming after him were really better than he was. He made no pretense to a humility he did not possess. In his heart of hearts he constantly underestimated himself, and overestimated others.

He really believed that God would use other men in a larger measure than he had been used. Mr. Moody loved to keep himself in the background. At his conventions at Northfield, or anywhere else, he would push the other men to the front and, if he could, have them do all the preaching—McGregor, Campbell Morgan, Andrew Murray, and the rest of them. The only way we could get him to take any part in the program was to get up in the convention and move that we hear D. L. Moody at the next meeting. He continually put himself out of sight.

Oh, how many a man has been full of promise and God has used him, and then the man thought that he was the whole thing and God was compelled to set him aside! I believe more promising workers have gone on the rocks through self-sufficiency and self-esteem than through any other cause. I can look back for forty years, or more, and think of many men who are now wrecks or derelicts who at one time the world thought were going to be something great. But they have disappeared entirely from the public view. Why? Because of overestimation of self. Oh, the men and women who have been put aside because they began to think that they were somebody, that they were "IT," and therefore God was compelled to set them aside.

I remember a man with whom I was closely associated in a great movement in this country. We were having a most successful convention in Buffalo, and he was greatly elated. As we walked down the street together to one of the meetings one day, he said to me: "Torrey, you and I are the most important men in Christian work in this country," or words to that effect. I replied: "John, I am sorry to hear you say that; for as I read my Bible I find man after man who had accomplished great things whom God had to set aside because of his sense of his own importance." And God set that man aside also from that time. I think he is still living, but no one ever hears of him, or has heard of him for years.

God used D. L. Moody, I think, beyond any man of his day; but it made no difference how much God used him, he never was puffed up. One day, speaking to me of a great New York preacher, now dead, Mr. Moody said: "He once did a very foolish thing, the most foolish thing that I ever knew a man, ordinarily so wise as he was, to do. He came up to me at the close of a little talk I had given and said: 'Young man, you have made a great address tonight.'" Then Mr. Moody continued: "How foolish of him to have said that! It almost turned my head." But, thank God, it did not turn his head, and even when pretty much all the ministers in England, Scotland and Ireland, and many of the English bishops were ready to follow D. L. Moody wherever he led, even then it never turned his head one bit. He would get down on his face before God, knowing he was human, and ask God to empty him of all self-sufficiency. And God did.

Oh, men and women! especially young men and young women, perhaps God is beginning to use you; very likely people are saying: "What a wonderful gift he has as a Bible teacher, what power he has as a preacher, for such a young man!" Listen: get down upon your face before God. I believe here lies one of the most dangerous snares of the Devil. When the Devil cannot discourage a man, he approaches him on another tack, which he knows is far worse in its results; he puffs him up by whispering in his ear: "You are the leading evangelist of the day. You are the man who will sweep everything before you. You are the coming man. You are the D. L. Moody of the day"; and if you listen to him, he will ruin you. The entire shore of the history of Christian workers is strewn with the wrecks of gallant vessels that were full of promise a few years ago, but these men became puffed up and were driven on the rocks by the wild winds of their own raging self-esteem.

5. His Entire Freedom from the Love of Money

The fifth secret of D. L. Moody's continual power and usefulness was his entire freedom from the love of money. Mr. Moody might have been a wealthy man, but money had no charms for him. He loved to gather money for God's work; he refused to accumulate money for himself. He told me during the World's Fair that if he had taken, for himself, the royalties on the hymnbooks which he had published, they would have amounted, at that time, to a million dollars. But Mr. Moody refused to touch the money. He had a perfect right to take it, for he was responsible for the publication of the books and it was his money that went into the publication of the first of them.

Mr. Sankey had some hymns that he had taken with him to England and he wished to have them published. He went to a publisher (I think Morgan & Scott) and they declined to publish them, because, as they said, Philip Phillips had recently been over and published a hymnbook and it had not done well. However, Mr. Moody had a little money and he said that he would put it into the publication of these hymns in cheap form; and he did. The hymns had a most remarkable and unexpected sale; they were then published in book form and large profits accrued. The financial results were offered to

Mr. Moody, but he refused to touch them. "But," it was urged on him, "the money belongs to you"; but he would not touch it.

Mr. Fleming H. Revell was at the time treasurer of the Chicago Avenue Church, commonly known as the Moody Tabernacle. Only the basement of this new church building had been completed, funds having been exhausted. Hearing of the hymnbook situation Mr. Revell suggested, in a letter to friends in London, that the money be given for completion of this building, and it was. Afterwards, so much money came in that it was given, by the committee into whose hands Mr. Moody put the matter, to various Christian enterprises.

In a certain city to which Mr. Moody went in the latter years of his life, and where I went with him, it was publicly announced that Mr. Moody would accept no money whatever for his services. Now, in point of fact, Mr. Moody was dependent, in a measure, upon what was given him at various services; but when this announcement was made, Mr. Moody said nothing, and left that city without a penny's compensation for the hard work he did there; and, I think, he paid his own hotel bill. And yet a minister in that very city came out with an article in a paper, which I read, in which he told a fairy tale of the financial demands that Mr. Moody made upon them, which story I knew personally to be absolutely untrue. Millions of dollars passed into Mr. Moody hands, but they passed through; they did not stick to his fingers.

This is the point at which many an evangelist makes shipwreck, and his great work comes to an untimely end. The love of money on the part of some evangelists has done more to discredit evangelistic work in our day, and to lay many an evangelist on the shelf, than almost any other cause.

While I was away on my recent tour I was told by one of the most reliable ministers in one of our eastern cities of a campaign conducted by one who has been greatly used in the past. (Do not imagine, for a moment, that I am speaking of Billy Sunday, for I am not; this same minister spoke in the highest terms of Mr. Sunday and of a campaign which he conducted in a city where this minister was a pastor.) This evangelist of whom I now speak came to a city for a united evangelistic campaign and was supported by fifty-three churches. The minister who told me about the matter was himself chairman of the Finance Committee.

The evangelist showed such a longing for money and so deliberately violated the agreement he had made before coming to the city and so insisted upon money being gathered for him in other ways than he had himself prescribed in the original contract, that this minister threatened to resign from the Finance Committee. He was, however, persuaded to remain to avoid a scandal. "As the total result of the three weeks' campaign there were only twenty-four clear decisions," said my friend; "and after it was over the ministers got together and by a vote with but one dissenting voice, they agreed to send a letter to this evangelist telling him frankly that they were done with him and with his methods of evangelism forever, and that they felt it their duty to warn other cities against him and his methods and the results of his work." Let us lay the lesson to our hearts and take warning in time.

6. His Consuming Passion for the Salvation of the Lost

The sixth reason why God used D. L. Moody was because of his consuming passion for the salvation of the lost. Mr. Moody made the resolution, shortly after he himself was saved, that he would never let twenty-four hours pass over his head without speaking to at least one person about his soul. His was a very busy life, and sometimes he would forget his resolution until the last hour, and sometimes he would get out of bed, dress, go out and talk to someone about his soul in order that he might not let one day pass without having definitely told at least one of his fellow-mortals about his need and the Savior who could meet it.

One night Mr. Moody was going home from his place of business. It was very late, and it suddenly occurred to him that he had not spoken to one single person that day about accepting Christ. He said to himself: "Here's a day lost. I have not spoken to anyone today and I shall not see anybody at this late hour." But as he walked up the street he saw a man standing under a lamppost. The man was a perfect stranger to him, though it turned out afterwards the man knew who Mr. Moody was. He stepped up to this stranger and said: "Are you a Christian?" The man replied: "That is none of your business, whether I am a Christian or not. If you were not a sort of a preacher I would knock you into the gutter for your impertinence." Mr. Moody said a few earnest words and passed on.

The next day that man called upon one of Mr. Moody's prominent business friends and said to him: "That man Moody of yours over on the North Side is doing more harm than he is good. He has got zeal without knowledge. He stepped up to me last night, a perfect stranger, and insulted me. He asked me if I were a Christian, and I told him it was none of his business and if he were not a sort of a preacher I would knock him into the gutter for his impertinence. He is doing more harm than he is good. He has got zeal without knowledge." Mr. Moody's friend sent for him and said: "Moody, you are doing more harm than you are good; you've got zeal without knowledge: you insulted a friend of mine on the street last night. You went up to him, a perfect stranger, and asked him if he were a Christian, and he tells me if you had not been a sort of a preacher he would have knocked you into the gutter for your impertinence. You are doing more harm than you are good; you have got zeal without knowledge."

Mr. Moody went out of that man's office somewhat crestfallen. He wondered if he were not doing more harm than he was good, if he really had zeal without knowledge. (Let me say, in passing, it is far better to have zeal without knowledge than it is to have knowledge without zeal. Some men and women are as full of knowledge as an egg is of meat; they are so deeply versed in Bible truth that they can sit in criticism on the preachers and give the preachers pointers, but they have so little zeal that they do not lead one soul to Christ in a whole year.)

Weeks passed by. One night Mr. Moody was in bed when he heard a tremendous pounding at his front door. He jumped out of bed and rushed to the door. He thought the house was on fire. He thought the man would break down the door. He opened the door and there stood this man. He said: "Mr. Moody, I have not had a good night's sleep since that night you spoke to me under the lamppost, and I have come around at this unearthly hour of the night for you to tell me what I have to do to be saved." Mr. Moody took him in and told him what to do to be saved. Then he accepted Christ, and when the Civil War broke out, he went to the front and laid down his life fighting for his country.

Another night, Mr. Moody got home and had gone to bed before it occurred to him that he had not spoken to a soul that day about accepting Christ. "Well," he said to himself, "it is no good getting up now; there will be nobody on the street at this hour of the night." But he got up, dressed and went to the front door. It was pouring rain. "Oh," he said, "there will be no one out in this pouring rain. Just then he heard the patter of a man's feet as he came down the street, holding an umbrella over his head. Then Mr. Moody darted out and rushed up to the man and said: "May I share the shelter of your umbrella?" "Certainly," the man replied. Then Mr. Moody said: "Have you any shelter in the time of storm?" and preached Jesus to him. Oh, men and women, if we were as full of zeal for the salvation of souls as that, how long would it be before the whole country would be shaken by the power of a mighty, God-sent revival?

One day in Chicago—the day after the elder Carter Harrison was shot, when his body was lying in state in the City Hall—Mr. Moody and I were riding up Randolph Street together in a streetcar right alongside of the City Hall. The car could scarcely get through because of the enormous crowds waiting to get in and view the body of Mayor Harrison. As the car tried to push its way through the crowd, Mr. Moody turned to me and said: "Torrey, what does this mean?" "Why," I said, "Carter Harrison's body lies there in the City Hall and these crowds are waiting to see it."

Then he said: "This will never do, to let these crowds get away from us without preaching to them; we must talk to them. You go and hire Hooley's Opera House (which was just opposite the City Hall) for the whole day." I did so. The meetings began at nine o'clock in the morning, and we had one continuous service from that hour until six in the evening, to reach those crowds.

Mr. Moody was a man on fire for God. Not only was he always "on the job" himself but he was always getting others to work as well. He once invited me down to Northfield to spend a month there with the schools, speaking first to one school and then crossing the river to the other. I was obliged to use the ferry a great deal; it was before the present bridge was built at that point.

One day he said to me: "Torrey, did you know that that ferryman that ferries you across every day was unconverted?" He did not tell me to speak to him, but I knew what he meant. When some days later it was told him that the ferryman was saved, he was exceedingly happy.

Once, when walking down a certain street in Chicago, Mr. Moody stepped up to a man, a perfect stranger to him, and said: "Sir, are you a Christian?" "You mind your own business," was the reply. Mr. Moody replied: "This is my business." The man said, "Well, then, you must be Moody." Out in Chicago they used to call him in those early days "Crazy Moody," because day and night he was speaking to everybody he got a chance to speak to about being saved.

One time he was going to Milwaukee, and in the seat that he had chosen sat a traveling man. Mr. Moody sat down beside him and immediately began to talk with him. "Where are you going?" Mr. Moody asked. When told the name of the town he said: "We will soon be there; we'll have to get down to business at once. Are you saved?" The man said that he was not, and Mr. Moody took out his Bible and there on the train showed him the way of salvation. Then he said: "Now, you must take Christ." The man did; he was converted right there on the train.

Most of you have heard, I presume, the story President Wilson used to tell about D. L. Moody. Ex-President Wilson said that he once went into a barber shop and took a chair next to the one in which D. L. Moody was sitting, though he did not know that Mr. Moody was there. He had not been in the chair very long before, as ex-President Wilson phrased it, he "knew there was a personality in the other chair," and he began to listen to the conversation going on; he heard Mr. Moody tell the barber about the Way of Life, and President Wilson said, "I have never forgotten that scene to this day." When Mr. Moody was gone, he asked the barber who he was; when he was told that it was D. L. Moody, President Wilson said: "It made an impression upon me I have not yet forgotten."

On one occasion in Chicago Mr. Moody saw a little girl standing on the street with a pail in her hand. He went up to her and invited her to his Sunday school, telling her what a pleasant place it was. She promised to go the following Sunday, but she did not do so. Mr. Moody watched for her for weeks, and then one day he saw her on the street again, at some distance from him. He started toward her, but she saw him too and started to run away. Mr. Moody followed her. Down she went one street, Mr. Moody after her; up she went another street, Mr. Moody after her, through an alley, Mr. Moody still following; out on another street, Mr. Moody after her; then she dashed into a saloon and Mr. Moody dashed after her. She ran out the back door and up a flight of stairs, Mr. Moody still following; she dashed into a room, Mr. Moody following; she threw herself under the bed and Mr. Moody reached under the bed and pulled her out by the foot, and led her to Christ.

He found that her mother was a widow who had once seen better circumstances, but had gone down until now she was living over this saloon. She had several children. Mr. Moody led the mother and all the family to Christ. Several of the children were prominent members of the Moody Church until they moved away, and afterwards became prominent in churches elsewhere. This particular child, whom he pulled from underneath the bed, was, when I was the pastor of the Moody Church, the wife of one of the most prominent officers in the church.

Only two or three years ago, as I came out of a ticket office in Memphis, Tennessee, a fine-looking young man followed me. He said: "Are you not Dr. Torrey?" I said, "Yes." He said: "I am so and so." He was the son of this woman. He was then a traveling man, and an officer in the church where he lived. When Mr. Moody pulled that little child out from under the bed by the foot he was pulling a whole family into the Kingdom of God, and eternity alone will reveal how many succeeding generations he was pulling into the Kingdom of God.

D. L. Moody's consuming passion for souls was not for the souls of those who would be helpful to him in building up his work here or elsewhere; his love for souls knew no class limitations. He was no respecter of persons; it might be an earl or a duke or it might be an uneducated boy on the street; it was all the same to him; there was a soul to save and he did what lay in his power to save that soul.

A friend once told me that the first time he ever heard of Mr. Moody was when Mr. Reynolds of Peoria told him that he once found Mr. Moody sitting in one of the squatters' shanties that used to be in that part of the city toward the lake, which was then called, "The Sands," with a boy on his knee, a tallow candle in one hand and a Bible in the other, and Mr. Moody was spelling out the words (for at that time the boy could not read very well) of certain verses of Scripture, in an attempt to lead that boy to Christ.

Oh, young men and women and all Christian workers, if you and I were on fire for souls like that, how long would it be before we had a revival? Suppose that tonight the fire of God falls and fills our hearts, a burning fire that will send us out all over the country, and across the water to China, Japan, India and Africa, to tell lost souls the way of salvation!

7. Definitely Endued with Power from on High

The seventh thing that was the secret of why God used D. L. Moody was that he had a very definite enduement with power from on High, a very clear and definite baptism with the Holy Ghost. Moody knew he had "the baptism with the Holy Ghost"; he had no doubt about it. In his early days he was a great hustler; he had a tremendous desire to do something, but he had no real power. He worked very largely in the energy of the flesh.

But there were two humble Free Methodist women who used to come over to his meetings in the Y.M.C.A. One was "Auntie Cook" and the other, Mrs. Snow. (I think her name was not Snow at that time.) These two women would come to Mr. Moody at the close of his meetings and say: "We are praying for you." Finally, Mr. Moody became somewhat nettled and said to them one night: "Why are you praying for me? Why don't you pray for the unsaved?" They replied: "We are praying that you may get the power." Mr. Moody did not know what that meant, but he got to thinking about it, and then went to these women and said: "I wish you would tell me what you mean"; and they told him about the definite baptism with the Holy Ghost. Then he asked that he might pray with them and not they merely pray for him.

Auntie Cook once told me of the intense fervor with which Mr. Moody prayed on that occasion. She told me in words that I scarcely dare repeat, though I have never forgotten them. And he not only prayed with them, but he also prayed alone.

Not long after, one day on his way to England, he was walking up Wall Street in New York; (Mr. Moody very seldom told this and I almost hesitate to tell it) and in the midst of the bustle and hurry of that city his prayer was answered; the power of God fell upon him as he walked up the street and he had to hurry off to the house of a friend and ask that he might have a room by himself, and in that room he stayed alone for hours; and the Holy Ghost came upon him, filling his soul with such joy that at last he had to ask God to withhold His hand, lest he die on the spot from very joy. He went out from that place with the power of the Holy Ghost upon him, and when he got to London (partly through the prayers of a bedridden saint in Mr. Lessey's church), the power of God wrought through him mightily in North London, and hundreds were added to the churches; and that was what led to his being invited over to the wonderful campaign that followed in later years.

Time and again Mr. Moody would come to me and say: "Torrey, I want you to preach on the baptism with the Holy Ghost." I do not know how many times he asked me to speak on that subject. Once, when I had been invited to preach in the Fifth Avenue Presbyterian Church, New York (invited at Mr. Moody's suggestion; had it not been for his suggestion the invitation would never have been extended to me), just before I started for New York, Mr. Moody drove up to my house and said: "Torrey, they want you to preach at the Fifth Avenue Presbyterian Church in New York. It is a great big church, cost a million dollars to build it." Then he continued: "Torrey, I just want to ask one thing of you. I want to tell you what to preach about. You will preach that sermon of yours on 'Ten Reasons Why I Believe the Bible to Be the Word of God' and your sermon on 'The Baptism With the Holy Ghost.'"

Time and again, when a call came to me to go off to some church, he would come up to me and say: "Now, Torrey, be sure and preach on the baptism with the Holy Ghost." I do not know how many times he said that to me. Once I asked him: "Mr. Moody, don't you think I have any sermons but those two: 'Ten Reasons Why I Believe the Bible to Be the Word of God' and 'The Baptism With the Holy Ghost'?" "Never mind that," he replied, "you give them those two sermons."

Once he had some teachers at Northfield—fine men, all of them, but they did not believe in a definite baptism with the Holy Ghost for the individual. They believed that every child of God was baptized with the Holy Ghost, and they did not believe in any special baptism with the Holy Ghost for the individual. Mr. Moody came to me and said: "Torrey, will you come up to my house after the meeting tonight and I will get those men to come, and I want you to talk this thing out with them."

Of course, I very readily consented, and Mr. Moody and I talked for a long time, but they did not altogether see eye to eye with us. And when they went, Mr. Moody signaled me to remain for a few moments. Mr. Moody sat there with his chin on his breast, as he so often sat when he was in deep thought; then he looked up and said: "Oh, why will they split hairs? Why don't they see that this is just the one thing that they themselves need? They are good teachers, they are wonderful teachers, and I am so glad to have them here; but why will they not see that the baptism with the Holy Ghost is just the one touch that they themselves need?"

I shall never forget the eighth of July, 1894, to my dying day. It was the closing day of the Northfield Students' Conference—the gathering of the students from the eastern colleges. Mr. Moody had asked me to preach on Saturday night and Sunday morning on the baptism with the Holy Ghost. On Saturday night I had spoken about, "The Baptism With the Holy Ghost: What It Is; What It Does; the Need of It and the Possibility of It." On Sunday morning I spoke on "The Baptism With the Holy Spirit: How to Get It." It was just exactly twelve o'clock when I finished my morning sermon, and I took out my watch and said: "Mr. Moody has invited us all to go up to the mountain at three o'clock this afternoon to pray for the power of the Holy Spirit. It is three hours to three o'clock. Some of you cannot wait three hours. You do not need to wait. Go to your rooms; go out into the woods; go to your tent; go anywhere where you can get alone with God and have this matter out with Him."

At three o'clock we all gathered in front of Mr. Moody's mother's house (she was then still living), and then began to pass down the lane, through the gate, up on the mountainside. There were four hundred and fifty-six of us in all; I know the number because Paul Moody counted us as we passed through the gate.

After a while Mr. Moody said: "I don't think we need to go any further; let us sit down here." We sat down on stumps and logs and on the ground. Mr. Moody said: "Have any of you students anything to say?" I think about seventy-five of them arose, one after the other, and said: "Mr. Moody, I could not wait till three o'clock; I have been alone with God since the morning service, and I believe I have a right to say that I have been baptized with the Holy Spirit."

When these testimonies were over, Mr. Moody said: "Young men, I can't see any reason why we shouldn't kneel down here right now and ask God that the Holy Ghost may fall upon us just as definitely as He fell upon the apostles on the Day of Pentecost. Let us pray." And we did pray, there on the mountainside. As we had gone up the mountainside heavy clouds had been gathering, and just as we began to pray those clouds broke and the raindrops began to fall through the overhanging pines. But there was another cloud that had been gathering over Northfield for ten days, a cloud big with the mercy and grace and power of God; and as we began to pray our prayers seemed to pierce that cloud and the Holy Ghost fell upon us. Men and women, that is what we all need the Baptism with the Holy Ghost.

ONLY ONE LIFE
by C. T. Studd

C. T. Studd (1860–1931) was converted under the ministry of D. L. Moody and achieved fame as an all-England cricketer at Cambridge. He was influential in helping establish the Student Volunteer Movement to recruit young people for world missions, and he later served as a missionary in China, India, and Africa.

Two little lines I heard one day,
Traveling along life's busy way;
Bringing conviction to my heart,
And from my mind would not depart;
Only one life, 'twill soon be past,
Only what's done for Christ will last.
Only one life, yes only one,
Soon will its fleeting hours be done;
Then, in 'that day' my Lord to meet,
And stand before His Judgement seat;

Only one life, 'twill soon be past,
Only what's done for Christ will last.

Only one life, the still small voice,
Gently pleads for a better choice
Bidding me selfish aims to leave,
And to God's holy will to cleave;
Only one life, 'twill soon be past,
Only what's done for Christ will last.

Only one life, a few brief years,
Each with its burdens, hopes, and fears;
Each with its clays I must fulfill,
living for self or in His will;
Only one life, 'twill soon be past,
Only what's done for Christ will last.

When this bright world would tempt me sore,
When Satan would a victory score;
When self would seek to have its way,
Then help me Lord with joy to say;
Only one life, 'twill soon be past,
Only what's done for Christ will last.

Give me Father, a purpose deep,
In joy or sorrow Thy word to keep;
Faithful and true what e'er the strife,
Pleasing Thee in my daily life;
Only one life, 'twill soon be past,
Only what's done for Christ will last.

Oh let my love with fervor burn,

And from the world now let me turn;
Living for Thee, and Thee alone,
Bringing Thee pleasure on Thy throne;
Only one life, 'twill soon be past,
Only what's done for Christ will last.
Only one life, yes only one,
Now let me say, "Thy will be done";
And when at last I'll hear the call,
I know I'll say "twas worth it all";
Only one life, 'twill soon be past,
Only what's done for Christ will last.

MY CONSECRATION AS A CHRISTIAN

by John G. Lake[1]

John G. Lake (1870–1935) was born in Canada and became a leader in the Pentecostal movement of the early twentieth century. He is best remembered for his powerful ministry in South Africa and for twenty years of evangelistic work in the United States, during which he established many healing rooms to minister to the sick.

> I, this day, consecrate my entire life to glorify my Heavenly Father by my obedience to the principles of Jesus Christ through the power of the Holy Spirit. All my effort from now on will be directed in an effort to demonstrate the righteousness of God in whatsoever I may be engaged.

Principle 1

All the things earthly that I possess shall not be considered my own, but belonging to my Heavenly Father, and shall be held in trust by me to be used and directed by the wisdom of the Spirit of God, as the law of love of men as Christ loved them may dictate.

If at any time God should raise up men wiser than myself, I will gladly commit all to their use and turn over all my possessions to them for distribution.

If at any time in my life I should be engaged in any earthly business and should employ men to aid me in conducting it, I shall reward them justly and equally, comparing their own energy expended with my own after adding a sufficient amount to my own to cover all risk that may be involved in the operation of my business.

I shall consider my employees my equals with rights to the blessings of nature and life equal to my own. I shall not strive to elevate myself to a position of comfort above the rest of my employees and shall direct all my efforts to bring all mankind to an equal plane, where all enjoy the comforts of life and fellowship together.

Principle 2

I shall not cease to cry to God and implore Him to deliver mankind from the effects of sin so long as sin lasts, but shall cooperate with God in the redemption of mankind.

I will have seasons of prayer and fasting in behalf of mankind, weeping and bewailing their lost condition and imploring God to grant them repentance unto life as the Spirit of God may lead me.

Principle 3

I shall live my life in meekness, never defending my own personal rights, but shall leave all judgment to God Who judges righteously and rewards according to their works.

I shall not render evil for evil or railing for railing, but shall bless all and do good to enemies in return for evil.

By God's grace I shall keep all hardness and harshness out of my life and actions, but shall be gentle and unassuming, not professing above what God has imparted to me, nor lifting myself above my brethren.

Principle 4

> I shall consider righteous acts as more necessary to life and happiness than food and drink, and not let myself be bribed or coerced into any unrighteous action for earthly consideration.

Principle 5

> By God's grace I will always be merciful, forgiving those who have transgressed against me and endeavoring to correct the ills of humanity instead of merely punishing them for their sins.

Principle 6

I shall not harbor any impure thoughts in my mind, but shall endeavor to make every act uplifting.

I shall regard my procreative organs sacred and holy and never use them for any purpose other than that which God created them for.

I shall regard the home as sacred and always guard my actions in the presence of the opposite sex, so as not to cause a man and his wife to break their vows to one another. I shall be chaste with the opposite sex who are married, considering them as sisters. I shall be careful not to cause them undue pain by playing on their affections.

Principle 7

I will always strive to be a peacemaker. First, by being peaceful myself and avoiding all unfruitful contentions, and treating all with justice and regarding their rights and their free agency, never trying to force any to my point of view.

If I should offend anyone knowingly, I shall immediately apologize.

> I will not scatter evil reports about any person and so try to defame their character, or repeat things that I am not certain of being true.
>
> I will strive to remove the curse of strife among brethren by acting as a peacemaker.

Principle 8

> I shall not become discouraged when I am persecuted on account of the righteousness mentioned above nor murmur on account of any suffering I undergo, but shall gladly give my life rather than depart from this high standard of life, rejoicing because I know I have a great reward in Heaven.
>
> I shall strive to make the above principles the ideals of all the world and give my life and energy to see mankind get the power from God to practice the same.

Note

1. John G. Lake, *Adventures in God* (Shippensburg, PA: Harrison House, 1981), 121-125. Copyright © 1981 by Harrison House, Inc. All rights reserved. Used by permission of Destiny Image Publishers., Shippensburg PA, 17257.

Appendix G

MEET YOUR MENTORS

Thomas á Kempis (1380–1471) wrote *The Imitation of Christ*, long considered to be the best-selling Christian book of all time after the Bible.

Augustine of Hippo (354–430), a notable theologian and influential Bishop based in northern Africa who authored *The City of God* during the demise of the Roman Empire.

William Barclay (1907–1978), a Scottish New Testament scholar and commentator, is best remembered for his outstanding work, *Daily Study Bible*.

Richard Baxter (1615–1691), a leading Puritan minister, authored *The Saints Everlasting Rest* and dozens of other notable works.

Dietrich Bonhoeffer (1906–1945), a founding leader of the Confessing Church in Germany, a group that stood in opposition to Hitler and his policies, was eventually imprisoned and put to death. Bonhoeffer is best remembered for *The Cost of Discipleship* and *Letters from Prison*.

Catherine Booth (1829–1890) is remembered as "the mother of the Salvation Army." A powerful preacher in her own right, she co-founded that organization with her husband, William.

William Booth (1829–1912) was the first "general" of the Salvation Army. This highly evangelistic ministry targeted the poorest of the poor in the slums of East London. Today, the Salvation Army serves in 130 countries.

E. M. Bounds (1835–1913) initially practiced law but stepped into gospel ministry in his mid-twenties. He ultimately wrote eleven books, nine of which were focused on prayer.

Phillips Brooks (1835–1893), an Episcopal bishop in Boston, authored the famous hymn, "O Little Town of Bethlehem."

Thomas Brooks (1608–1680) was a seventeenth century non-conformist Puritan preacher from England. The author of several books, Brooks also preached in front of the House of Commons in 1648.

Oswald Chambers (1874–1917) was a Scottish minister who was brought to the Lord under Spurgeon's ministry. Chambers died while ministering to British troops in Egypt, and his most famous work, *My Upmost for His Highest*, was compiled by his wife from his notes and published after his death.

W. A. Criswell (1909–2002) is best known for having served as the pastor of First Baptist Church of Dallas for fifty years. He also served for two years as the president of the Southern Baptist Convention and wrote more than fifty books.

Jonathan Edwards (1703–1758) is considered by many to be America's first and greatest theologian. A Puritan pastor from New England, Edwards' name is closely associated with America's first great awakening. A prolific writer, his work, *A Surprising Narrative of the Surprising Work of God*, provides tremendous insights into the nature of revival.

Elisabeth Elliot (1926–2015) was married to Jim Elliot, the missionary who was killed with four others while trying to reach the Huaorani people of Ecuador. Elisabeth later went as a missionary to serve the very people who killed her husband. She was also a prolific author.

Charles Finney (1792–1875) was trained as a lawyer but surrendered to preach the gospel after a conversion experience. He is considered to be one of the greatest evangelists in American history, and he led much of the revival in the northeastern part of the United States in what is called its Second Great Awakening. He is the author of many works, including *Lectures on Revival*.

Donald Gee (1891–1966) was often referred to as "The Apostle of Balance." Born in England, Gee was a Pentecostal pioneer in the twentieth century and wrote nearly thirty books.

S. D. Gordon (1859–1936) was involved in the YMCA before traveling through Europe and Asia as a lecturer. He is best remembered for his "Quiet Talks" series which sold more than 1.5 million copies.

Billy Graham (1918–2018) skyrocketed to fame in 1949 and became known as "America's Evangelist." Graham preached the gospel to more people in person than anyone else in history—nearly 215 million people in more than 185 countries and territories. He is also the author of thirty-three books.

Gregory of Nazianzus (329– 390) was an early Christian monk and minister from the Cappadocian region of modern-day Turkey. He was an eloquent preacher and scholarly writer.

Gregory the Great (540–604) stepped into a leadership role in Rome at a very critical time in that city's history. A humble man, Gregory would only refer to himself as a "servant of the servants of God."

To provide guidance and godly counsel to ministers in his time, Gregory wrote *The Book of Pastoral Rule,* which is loaded with rich insights for those serving God.

Vance Havner (1901–1986) was a tremendously quotable Baptist preacher who ministered for more than seventy years. In demand as a preacher, he spoke in countless churches, conferences, and Bible colleges across the country.

Carl F. H. Henry (1913–2003) was one of the founders of Fuller Theological Seminary in Pasadena, California, as well as the first editor of the magazine, *Christianity Today.* He was considered to be one of the leading spokespersons for the evangelical movement in the twentieth century.

Matthew Henry (1662–1714) is best remembered for the Bible commentary bearing his name. He was a Presbyterian minister, serving two congregations.

John Henry Jowett (1863–1923) was an English minister known as a dynamic and powerful preacher. As a pastor, he served both the Fifth Avenue Presbyterian Church in New York City and the Westminster Chapel in London.

Gordon Lindsay (1906–1973) was an evangelist in the 1930s and later served as an organizer, coordinator, and stabilizer for the healing movement. He headed up the organization known as "The Voice of Healing" and later founded "Christ for the Nations" along with his wife, Freda.

C. S. Lewis (1898–1963) authored more than twenty-five Christian works. He was known and respected as a professor at Oxford and Cambridge Universities in England.

Martin Luther (1483–1546) is synonymous with the Protestant Reformation. A German monk, Luther was grieved by the practice of indulgences and nailed his ninety-five theses to the door of the Castle Church in Wittenberg in 1517. A pastor and professor, Luther is also remembered for his emphasis on justification by faith. In addition to numerous other written works, Luther translated the New Testament into the common language of the people during his time in exile.

Alexander Maclaren (1826–1910) was a prolific author and eloquent preacher. He was awarded honorary doctorates from several British universities and served two terms as the president of the Baptist Union.

Peter Marshall (1902–1949) was born in Scotland but received his theological training in the United States. He became the pastor of the New York Avenue Presbyterian Church in Washington D.C. in 1937. He later served as Chaplain of the United States Senate.

G. Campbell Morgan (1863–1945) was considered to be the greatest Bible expositor of his day. Born in England, he was twice the pastor of Westminster Chapel in London. He produced more than seventy books throughout his lifetime and ministered extensively in the United States as well.

Robert Murray McCheyne (1813–1843) died before the age of thirty, and yet he had a powerful spiritual impact on Scotland during his brief ministry. McCheyne's life was documented through Andrew Bonar's work, *Memoir and Remains of Robert Murray McCheyne.*

Henrietta C. Mears (1890–1963) served as the director of Christian Education at the First Presbyterian Church of Hollywood, California, for thirty-five years. In addition to overseeing that program, Mears excelled at writing quality Christian curriculum and training up teachers. Under her leadership, their Sunday school grow from 450 to more than 6,500 during her first ten years in that position.

Dwight L. Moody (1837–1899) was the leading American evangelist of his day. His two primary bases of operation were Chicago (Moody Bible Church and Moody Bible Institute) and Northfield, Massachusetts (summer conferences as well as schools for young men and women).

John Mott (1865–1955) was an evangelical statesman who is most remembered for his work with the Student Volunteer Movement. His heart for missions is captured in the phrase, "The evangelization of the world in this generation."

Andrew Murray (1828–1917) was born of missionary parents in South Africa. Throughout his life he pastored, worked in Christian education, and traveled and spoke extensively. He left behind more than 240 books and tracts.

John Newton (1725–1807) was born in London and ultimately became the master of a slave ship. After conversion and deliverance from what he called a life of debauchery, Newton became a gospel minister and is best remembered as the author of the hymn, "Amazing Grace."

Johannes Oecolampadius (1482–1531) was an important figure in the Protestant Reformation, serving as a pastor and theologian. He was most closely associated with Ulrich Zwingli.

John Owen (1616–1683) is often considered to be the greatest theologian of the English Puritan movement. After serving as a pastor, he became Dean of Christ Church, Oxford's largest college.

Blaise Pascal (1623–1662) was a French Christian apologist, scientist, and mathematician. His book entitled *Pensées* (Thoughts) argued powerfully in favor of Christianity against rationalism and skepticism.

J. C. Ryle (1816–1900) was an Oxford-trained evangelical Christian leader from England. Ryle authored several books, and his successor called him "a man of granite with the heart of a child."

Charles C. Ryrie (1925–2016) was a long-term professor at Dallas Theological Seminary. In addition to authoring many books, his study Bible has sold more than 2 million copies.

Oswald Sanders (1902–1992) was the overseer of the China Inland Mission (now the Overseas Missionary Fellowship) and was a catalyst in launching new mission projects throughout East Asia. Sanders wrote more than forty books, including the classic, *Spiritual Leadership*.

Francis A. Schaeffer (1912–1984) was raised and pastored churches in the United States before moving to Switzerland and eventually founding an international study and ministry community in the Swiss Alps named L'Abri (shelter). Remembered as a Christian philosopher, Schaeffer authored more than twenty books.

A. B. Simpson (1843–1919) was a Presbyterian pastor from Canada. He eventually settled in New York and founded the Christian and Missionary Alliance, which focused on Jesus as Savior, Sanctifier, Healer, and Coming King.

Philip Jacob Spener (1635–1705) was a German Lutheran Pietist and the author of "Pia Desideria" ("Pious Desires"). Spener emphasized heartfelt devotion to God beyond a mere intellectual assent to correct doctrine.

Charles Spurgeon (1834–1892) is widely known as "The Prince of Preachers." The Metropolitan Tabernacle in London, where Spurgeon preached from 1861 until shortly before his death, held

6,000 people. In addition to being a prolific author, Spurgeon had a heart and program to train ministers for greater effectiveness.

James S. Stewart (1896–1990) was trained in Scotland in both theology and medicine. After pastoring three churches, he served as Chair of New Testament Language, Literature, and Theology at New College, Edinburgh University from 1947–1966. He also served as chaplain to Queen Elizabeth.

John Stott (1921–2011) was a key influencer relative to the historic Lausanne Covenant (1974) and the author of *Basic Christianity,* which has sold over three million copies in more than fifty languages. Highly influential in the evangelical movement of the twentieth century, Stott served as rector of All Souls Church in London for many years.

Hudson Taylor (1832–1905) is remembered for taking the gospel to the interior of China and founding the China Inland Mission, which grew to 225 missionaries in Taylor's day. The China Inland Missions is now known as Overseas Missionary Fellowship.

A. W. Tozer (1897–1963) was a pastor and author who wrote more than forty books. Two of the most famous are *The Pursuit of God* and *Knowledge of the Holy*.

Thomas E. Trask (1936–) served as the General Superintendent of the Assemblies of God from 1993–2007. Trask has spent over 65 years in ministry, 25 of which were devoted to the pastorate.

John Wesley (1703–1791) is known as the founder of Methodism. He traveled around 250,000 miles ministering God's word, much of that on horseback. When he died, there were 72,000 Methodists in England and an additional 43,000 adherents in America. He had preached 42,000 sermons and authored 250 books and pamphlets.

George Whitefield (1714–1770) was a contemporary of Wesley and considered to be the greatest preacher of that era. In addition to his powerful influence in England, Whitefield conducted seven preaching tours to the American colonies and is considered to be the spark of America's First Great Awakening.

Warren Wiersbe (1929–2019) was a prolific Bible teacher and author, having published more than 150 books. Among the many positions Wiersbe held throughout his ministry career, he was the pastor of the famous Moody Bible Church in Chicago from 1971–1978.

Bruce Wilkinson (1940–) is a Christian teacher who has authored more than sixty books. He also founded "Walk Through the Bible" and "Teach Every Nation" (TEN).

ABOUT THE AUTHOR

B ible teacher and author Tony Cooke graduated from RHEMA Bible Training Center in 1980 and received degrees from North Central University (Bachelor's in Church Ministries) and from Liberty University (Master's in Theological Studies/ Church History). Tony's passion for teaching the Bible has taken him to forty-seven states and thirty-three nations. Various titles have been translated and published in eight other languages. Tony and his wife, Lisa, reside in Broken Arrow, Oklahoma, and are the parents of two children.

Other books by Tony include:

Life After Death: Rediscovering Life After Loss of a Loved One

In Search of Timothy: Discovering and Developing Greatness in Church Staff and Volunteers

Grace, the DNA of God; Qualified: Serving God with Integrity and Finishing Your Course with Honor

Through the Storms: Help from Heaven When All Hell Breaks Loose

Your Place on God's Dream Team: The Making of Champions

The Work Book: What We Do Matters to God

Lift: Experiencing the Elevated Life.

Miracles and the Supernatural Throughout Church History

www.tonycooke.org

Connect with us on
[f] Facebook @ HarrisonHousePublishers
and [O] Instagram @ HarrisonHousePublishing
so you can stay up to date with news
about our books and our authors.

Visit us at **www.harrisonhouse.com**
for a complete product listing as well as
monthly specials for wholesale distribution.